HAND DELIVERED HOPE

HAND DELIVERED HOPE

JIMI COOK

*with Cristi Cook and
Grant Venable*

Trilogy Christian Publishers

A Wholly Owned Subsidiary of Trinity Broadcasting Network

2442 Michelle Drive

Tustin, CA 92780

Copyright © 2020 by James L. Cook

Front cover photo by Phomotso Makeke Cook, photojournalist

All Scripture quotations, unless otherwise noted, taken from THE HOLY BIBLE, NEW INTERNATIONAL VERSION®, NIV® Copyright © 1973, 1978, 1984, 2011 by Biblica, Inc.® Used by permission. All rights reserved worldwide.

Scripture quotations marked (KJV) taken from The Holy Bible, King James Version. Cambridge Edition: 1769.

All rights reserved, including the right to reproduce this book or portions thereof in any form whatsoever.

For information, address Trilogy Christian Publishing

Rights Department, 2442 Michelle Drive, Tustin, Ca 92780.

Trilogy Christian Publishing/ TBN and colophon are trademarks of Trinity Broadcasting Network.

For information about special discounts for bulk purchases, please contact Trilogy Christian Publishing.

Manufactured in the United States of America

Trilogy Disclaimer: The views and content expressed in this book are those of the author and may not necessarily reflect the views and doctrine of Trilogy Christian Publishing or the Trinity Broadcasting Network.

10 9 8 7 6 5 4 3 2 1

Library of Congress Cataloging-in-Publication Data is available.

ISBN 978-1-64773-194-6

ISBN 978-1-64773-195-3 (ebook)

Acknowledgements and Dedication

My greatest thanks go to God for blessing me with an amazing family, an amazing education, and an amazing opportunity to be part of a development aid organization that is focused on empowering "the least of these."(Matthew 25:35–40) I also want to profoundly thank my mother, Jane Gordon Cook, and my grandparents, Bob and "Archie" Gordon for raising me the way they did—they taught me everything about life and how to live and love and I will forever be grateful for them and their influences on me. Of course, none of this would have been possible without my incredible wife, Dr. Cristi Cook, who said *yes* to Rwanda, supported all my crazy ideas, works as hard as anyone on the builds, inspires girls and women all over the world, and loves, encourages, supports, and inspires me every day. I also want to thank my sisters, who have bought in to *BTCV* in so many ways and told so many people about what their "little brother" is doing. Knowing they are proud of me and believe in what we are doing means the world to me. Very special thanks to Brian and Dominique Anderson as well. We started this crazy adventure together and remain the best of friends. We have probably told our story a couple hundred times now and Brian always ends it with "Yeah, I'm not the best at talking on the phone" and I always end it with "Shut up, you're *awesome!*" I am extremely grateful for the help that Rita Zoey Chin provided in shaping the final content, style, and format of this book; she was a fantastic writing coach! Special thanks to Kylee, Matt, Stacie, and Ned for reading the "rough cuts" of this book and helping me make it read much better. Lastly, I want to thank Grant Venable, all of the *BTCV* board of directors and advisory council members, and all of the Changers all over the world who sacrifice their time, talents, funds, and hard, hard work to **be the change you wish to see in the world!** You all restore my faith in humanity, make this world a much better place, and inspire me to keep going.

This book is dedicated to our South African son, Phomotso "Motsy" Makeke Cook, and the millions of amazing kids like him who desperately want and profoundly deserve the opportunity for a quality education. Phomotso left this earth at the far-too-young age of twenty-three, two days before he was to officially receive his university degree in photojournalism—his lifelong dream. It is sad that he did not get to experience the symbolic culmination of his hard work and education, but he definitely accomplished all his goals and more, and has inspired so many people around the world to passionately pursue their dreams, to learn and grow each and every day, and to **be the change you wish to see in the world.** We are so proud of Phomotso for accomplishing the seemingly impossible, and he did it all because he dared to dream big dreams and tirelessly pursue them with a humble confidence that we all should aspire to.

In the wake of his unexpected and unexplained passing, so many people asked "What can I do for you?" Well, if you ever get to know me or finish this book, it will be no surprise that I responded by providing a bullet point checklist:

The Phomotso Makeke Cook To-Do List

- Make sure your eternal destiny is secure (John 3:16–17)
- Tell your kids "I love you" every day you are with them
- Don't put off the important things like time spent together
- Pour yourself into your dreams with Phomotso-level passion
- Take care of your family and friends
- Be truly present with people. Put your cell phone down and really talk to people and more importantly, really listen. (Phomotso was a great listener!)
- Take and share pictures
- Be the change you wish to see in the world
- Every once in a while, eat your salad last (this is a Phomotso thing)

Right after his passing, my sister, Janet, reminded me of a great Phomotso story. We had just exited a stage show at Animal Kingdom that was remarkable. She asked him, "What did you like best?"

With his eyes as big as saucers and a spring in his step he replied, "Everything!"

My dear friend, Jim Stannard, shared this great hymn with me:

"What God Hath Promised" by Annie Johnson Flint

God hath not promised skies always blue, flower strewn pathways, all our lives through

God hath not promised sun without rain, joy without sorrow, peace without pain

But God hath promised strength for the day, rest for the labor, light for the way

Grace for the trials, help from above, unfailing sympathy, undying love.

Our wish for you all is to have Phomotso's everything-is-the-best approach to life and to know God's undying love. Hopefully, this book will help with both.

Love, The Cooks

Jimi, Cristi, and "Motsy"

Foreword

It is rare to find a person who God has blessed with both wisdom and a passionate heart for serving His people. However, it's even rarer to see someone choosing every day to use those gifts, and living out the change they want to create. Dr. Jimi and his wife Dr. Cristi are examples of people who have decided to live an unprecedented life, running after their true purpose and empowering others around them.

Jimi has been a great friend and business partner over the years. He was instrumental in helping my brother Andy and I create the films *Woodlawn* and *I Can Only Imagine*. During these times, I knew he and Cristi traveled a lot for mission trips. In fact, I could never reach them via phone, because they were always in the middle of Africa or somewhere. I was not sure what type of work they were doing overseas, but I knew they were pouring their lives into it. When I read this memoir, I was blown away by the incredible things God has used them to do.

Reading Jimi's story brought me to tears, and I felt a strong emotional connection to the story. Specifically, I was captivated by the moment where Jimi outlines his calling moment. That really brought it home for me, as my journey has had a similar arc. The message of pursuing your divine calling rings so true in this book, and I believe that Jimi's words will be applicable to anyone, no matter what story they find themselves in.

As a storyteller, I thoroughly enjoyed the detail and imagery Jimi uses to share the triumphs and struggles he and Cristi have faced in their journey. Not only does he lay out the joyful times beautifully, but he also is unafraid to tell the raw truth in the difficult moments. Through it all, his philanthropic heart for education is undoubtedly inspiring. His organization, Be The Change Volunteers, has creatively sought out some of the most impactful ways to reach and help people around the world.

Jimi's story and BTCV's journey will personally challenge you to get off the bench. These stories will fill you with hope and a drive to go after your own unique calling. Jimi's life pushes us all to see the bigger picture and follow after the passion inside of us. I hope after reading this book, you are inspired just as I was to *be the change you want to see in the world*.

Onward!

Jon Erwin

Writer and Director

Preface: Why and How

"You must be the change you wish to see in the world!" —Mahatma Gandhi

Did you know that more than 260 million children around the world have no access to education?

Did you know that in most developing countries, school is not free? Students must pay for tuition, uniforms, books, lunches, and their teachers' salaries, meaning that for millions of children, especially girls, a formal education is never going to be an option.

Did you know that millions of children around the world do not complete their education because their schools do not have the facilities, books, or teachers to provide a quality education for them? Millions of children do not get an education because they are forced to work, because they are forced to become child soldiers, because they cannot pay for school, because of racism, because of violence, or simply because they are female.

Did you know that one out of every two children is in poverty and that 30,000 children die every day because of poverty? Did you know that one in five adults in the developing world cannot read or write? Did you know that illiteracy rates among women in the developing world exceed seventy percent?

I didn't.

Although I come from a long line of teachers, even though all of my immediate family members, and many of my extended family members, are or were teachers, despite the fact that I completed twenty-six years of formal education including two doctoral degrees, and my entire career in veterinary medicine and orthopaedic surgery has been at a university, I was pretty clueless about education. I have had a world-class education and I have publicly credited my education for my accomplishments freely and frequently. Education is very important to me. But, I never really knew how important it was to who I am and how I can, and should, impact the world around me until I went on this incredible journey of hand delivering hope through the power of education. The most amazing and surprising thing about this journey is that it all started with two words from a bunch of desperately poor orphans in a no-name village in Africa: "Books! Tuition!" they said.

As you will read in this book, those two words led to the most important education that I ever received. This book is all about that kind of education—learning about true joy, gaining wisdom from the young and the old, changing sympathy into empathy, and finding out what the most important, enduring, and meaningful things in life are—all from amazing people scattered throughout forgotten villages around the world. I believe their stories will inspire you, change you, and educate you in ways that you may not have thought possible—just like they did for me—and that you will use your new education to *be the change that you want to see in our world*. My promise to them and my promise to you is to try my very best to tell their stories in a way that provides you with the most important education you can receive—through their amazing stories of resilience, passion, and hope—stories that can awaken you, inspire you, and change your life forever.

The stories I am able to pass along in this book allowed me to see the faces of poverty—true, abject, no shoes, one set of clothes, no home, no guarantee of a meal every day, no clean water, disease and pain and death everywhere poverty. I have seen the faces of poverty and the faces of poverty are ... quite frankly ... beautiful!

Despite not having anything we would consider as the most basic components of "standard living," those in poverty see the joy of life and of living. They appreciate water, singing, holding a baby, tradition, culture, sunrises, sunsets, a fire, the moon and stars, a cup of tea, rain, lightning, and thunder, the written word, bicycles and family. They look you in the eye when they talk to you and they listen, really *listen* to other people. They don't start every sentence with "I" or end them with "me." They love to learn, experience, and take in new things, thoughts, and ideas. They care about others. They care about you.

And, if that was not enough to inspire you and bring you to tears, the poorest of the poor, those with nothing, are always the first to offer you food if you look hungry, water if you look thirsty, a hug if you look sad, a hand if you need help, and a big, beautiful straight from the soul smile that springs from real joy in being alive and deep faith in a higher purpose, in community, in each other. The Bible says "Blessed are the poor in spirit, for theirs is the Kingdom of Heaven" (Matthew 5:3 NIV). Whether you believe that or not, I can promise you that if you spend some time with the truly poor, the absolutely destitute, the beautiful poor, you will believe that they deserve the kingdom of heaven!

So, how can we help? How can we "be the change"? What can you do to make a dent in these huge problems, disparities, and barriers entrenched in poverty? That's what the stories in this book answer. From Zambian kids responding, "Books! Tuition!" to Rwandan spackle, Guatemalan playgrounds and Peruvian toilets to Indian caste-shattering, Papua New Guinean tattoos, and South African miracles, the answers always came back to education.

Did you know that education reduces infant mortality, reduces maternal death rates, reduces teen pregnancy, and reduces malaria and HIV? Did you know that education deters terrorism and war? Did you know that education makes it possible to get a job and a job is the way out of poverty? Did you know that you really can't "give" someone out of poverty, but you can help provide an opportunity for an education which is an opportunity for a job which is an opportunity for a way out of poverty?

I didn't.

But, this is what I have come to realize during ten years of education-focused development aid and this is why we seek out the poorest of the poor to try to let them see hope through the opportunity of education. Education is the salve for their wounds, the medication for their illnesses, the milk for their babies, the clean water for them to drink, the nourishment for their bodies, the clothes on their backs and the shoes on their feet. Education is the freedom from their oppressors, the key to their shackles, and the weapon to fend off their enemies. Education can and does change the world. It is powerful—even in the hands of just one person. Nelson Mandela, Martin Luther King Jr., Mother Teresa, Gandhi, Malala and almost any other world-changer you can think of credit education as the impetus, inspiration, avenue, or springboard that made their incredible accomplishments possible. With the power of education, it only takes one to change the world!

So, how did I get from "I didn't know" to running a school-building organization? Well, during the last few days of a trip we took to Zambia, we started asking the children in the village what we could do for them. Every single beautiful child from four years of age to young adults had the same answer. *Did they ask for Air Jordans? Fossil watches? iPods? Laptops? Designer clothes?* No, every single one of those beautiful children looked us straight in the eyes and said "Please send me books and money for tuition so that I can go to school!" Wow! Talk about stop-me-dead-in-my-tracks answers to my question. There I was—the one who was always-together-with-answers-for-everything—with my mouth hanging open and a stunned look on my face as if they had just sucker-punched me in the gut. I had planned on making promises to send them presents at Christmas time, which I would have done, feeling great about my generosity and "being done with the whole thing." Another good deed from the great American philanthropist and all-around great guy, Jimi Cook.

For a few bucks that I didn't really need anyway, I could feel great about myself and brag to all my friends about the kids I helped in Africa—yay me! But then they said "Books and tuition"—*come on, did they really say that? Is there some catch here? Can they sell the books for more than the shoes, watches, and iPods? Will they really use the money for tuition?* There has got to be some scam here! No scam—just kids who knew better than a guy with two doctoral degrees that education brings opportunity and opportunity brings hope. That's it, I was hooked. They got me at "books and tuition," and it was now my mission to find a way to make it happen for as many of these deserving students as I could in my lifetime.

So that's what this book is about—the stories we learned from amazing women, men, girls, and boys from around the world during our first ten years of trying to help change the world by using the most powerful weapon known to man—education—a weapon of opportunity, a weapon of change, a weapon of hope... hand delivered.

Kids in Zambia who replied, "Books! Tuition!"

Table of Contents

ZAMBIA 19
RWANDA 37
CAMBODIA 49
PAPUA NEW GUINEA 63
SOUTH AFRICA 75
NEPAL 97
ETHIOPIA 111
MALAWI 117
INDIA 131
KENYA 141
GUATEMALA 159
PERU 167
FULL CIRCLE 179

ZAMBIA

What you leave behind is not what is engraved in stone monuments, but what is woven into the lives of others!

—Pericles

I hung up the phone, walked to our midwestern American kitchen where my wife, Cristi, had just put down her phone, and I looked at her with a smirk of offended disgust and said, "I do *not* like that guy!" We had just completed the telephone interview that would decide whether we were worthy enough to give up two weeks of our lives, our entire vacation time from work, and spend about $3,500 each to be on Mr. Brian Anderson's Habitat for Humanity Global Village team to Zambia. Cristi, in her typical calm and not-rushing-to-judgment way, said "Yeah, he is not the greatest to talk to on the phone, but we just need to let it play out and see what happens—it will work out." Not only was Mr. Anderson—a Boston-raised insurance salesman living in Miami and fitting every one of the associated stereotypes in my mind—*not the greatest to talk to on the phone*, but he also didn't even tell us if we actually would be granted the privilege of sacrificing our time and money to be on his team. I was ready to tell him to take a long walk off a short Miami pier, but Cristi, and God, had other plans. Thank goodness, I listened to both this time. My life was about to change forever.

Fast forward six months, after Mr. Anderson decided we were in fact worthy for his team and we had saved money, read about Zambia, got 713 vaccinations (you will soon learn I exaggerate some things), convinced our families we were still sane and would likely come back alive, and made all of the necessary arrangements required for us to be gone and *incommunicado* for two full weeks, and Cristi and I were standing on the steps of the London Pavilion in Piccadilly Circus. This is where Team Zambia would meet up to head to Heathrow together to catch our flight to Africa. I still had a great deal of trepidation in going to a remote village in Zambia with this Anderson character as my leader, but I figured I was with Cristi, surely some of the other team members would be "cool," and I can do pretty much anything for two weeks. There we stood in the human chaos of London, partly lost in our own minds, partly lost in the crowd, and mostly lost in the anticipation of what might be in store for us.

We were looking over the massive crowd of tourists, artisans, street people, and business men and women as we were trying to pick out somebody that looked like a Miami-transplanted Bostonian insurance salesman (*how did we think we were going to find each other, again?*). Suddenly, we hear someone behind us say "Yoooo guyz must be da Cooks" and turned around to find this guy in a T-shirt, cargo shorts, and flip-flops smiling at us, arms spread wide, and eyebrows raised in a welcoming and adventurous way that seemed to say *"I am so glad and grateful to have you on this team and we are going to experience things 'normal people' can only imagine!"* Hmmm, I thought, *this must be one of the other team members—see I was right, there will be someone on the team who is cool—thank God*!

With both relief and interest coming over me, I replied, "Yes, I'm Jimi, this is Cristi, you must be on the team with us?" He said, "Yeh, I'm Brian, great to meet yooo, so glad yooo guyz are on this team!" *Whoa, dude, if you are Brian, our team leader, then who was that guy on the phone we talked to? I LOVE this guy!*

Cristi and I had decided to go on a Habitat build after I watched a special on Jimmy Carter and got really inspired by the "help up, not a hand out" and "sweat equity" principles of the organization. Since we both loved to travel and had "experiencing the world" in our blood, we decided that Habitat trips would be, and I quote (myself), *a really altruistic way for us to see the world*. Yep, a true do-gooder interested in a win-win—be the big man helping others while it was still really all about me. So, we looked at the website and found the Zambia build.

Zambia turned out to be everything a global mission trip should be. Difficult travel, crazy, scary situations and experiences, ridiculous living, working, and climate conditions... and the most beautiful, joy-filled, real, and amazing people to get to know, learn from, and serve. After Brian found us on the steps of the London Pavilion, we also found the rest of the team joining us there, found out two members of the team would meet us in Lusaka, made our way to Heathrow, and flew from London to Nairobi and Nairobi to Lusaka without a problem. En route, we learned a bit more about our team leader and the other team members with us.

Brian, while being the stereotypical Boston-born-and-bred Miami insurance salesman on the phone, was actually the stereotype of the rest of his story in person—big Catholic family, military veteran, and seasoned boots-on-the-ground humanitarian who cared deeply about family, modeled servant leadership, and would give you the shirt off his back, especially if you were helping him help others. He loved to talk as much as I did, so we got to know—and love—each other very quickly on our first long journey together.

The team also included Bennie, who spent a lot of his life as a street fighter to make ends meet and who Brian had taken under his wing and helped land a safer job as a security guard for Miami's Habitat for Humanity lumber and supplies yard. Picture an older version of Mr. T, but way tougher even without the mohawk or tattoos—definitely a guy you want on your team, especially on your first trip to the developing world.

We also met Maureen, who quickly became "Mo," a college student from Pittsburgh who had a heart for others, a heart for Africa, and an infectious, adventurous spirit that showed no fear, pre-judgment, or worry about what others thought. Hannah, an amazing young free spirit who had done Global Habitat before, taught English in a remote African school, and traveled the world before most people have their first real job, and had a deep spiritual presence that did not need words to be felt and appreciated. Derek, a just-finished-architect-school young professional, wanted a philanthropic adventure before starting "real life" and was strong, funny, and very laid back. Toby and Samantha, or Sam, a young couple from England, were in way over their heads, but wanted to be, and dealt with it all so well with grace, humor, humility and great British accents that made everything sound "brilliant." Then, there was

Carrie, a twenty-something Canadian, just getting over the end of a romance; another young British woman who was just about to start training for the constabulary; and a middle-aged couple from Arizona who watched the same Jimmy Carter show I did and made the same decision we did.

Upon arrival, I learned that the airlines lost my bag, so it looked like all I would have for two weeks on this Habitat for Humanity house-building project in remote sub-Saharan Africa was what I had on, what I had in my backpack, what I could find at a local market if there was time, and what I could borrow from my new best friend, Brian. Now, I am six-foot-three and Brian is five-foot-eight, and most Zambians I saw at the airport were neither, so the latter two options were not looking good.

Besides, we had a much bigger issue to deal with right away. Two of the American women on the team, who were over sixty years old, had met us after going on a safari. On the trip, they were robbed at knife-point, fending off the robbers by screaming at them. Both of our new team members were apparently completely undaunted by this pre-build calamity and ready to "just move on" to the project, which was completely amazing and very reassuring to me.

Unfortunately, one thing the robbers managed to grab was one of the women's passports. So that meant we had to go to the US Embassy in Lusaka to get her a new one. We also had to exchange all the money for the team's in-country transportation, lodging, food, and building materials, and we did not have much time. Mr. Anderson, gave his now-complete fourteen-member team the plan.

"Okay, Jimi and Cristi, you guys take the cash and we will drop you off in the market area to exchange the money—exchange it all for Zambian *kwacha*. The rest of you guys will go with me to the US Embassy and we will get Doris a new passport. Then, we will swing back by to pick up Jimi and Cristi and head to the village."

It sounded like a good plan and I didn't really question it...until we got off the bus in the market place and saw our only contacts in the country, our means of transportation, and our "safety net" drive away. Also, remember, I had only what I was wearing (a T-shirt and cargo shorts) and my passport, and Cristi had the same—in the rush, we also left our backpacks on the bus…that just drove away. And then there was the small matter of the *plastic bag stuffed with cash* that I was carrying in the middle of this marketplace teeming with people who apparently didn't have anything more pressing to do besides peer at us, the only two white people as far as the eye could see. Was this a set up? *Wait a minute, Boston-born, Miami "insurance salesman" who carries cash in a plastic bag?! We are going to die!*

Well, we figured if we were going to die, we might as well die trying, so we walked across the dusty dirt-and-gravel parking area of the market to the one bank that was there. Of course, it was in the center of the market, where the most people and the most attention were. There were people coming in and out of other shops, people milling about, people sitting on window sills, people sitting on the ground, people leaning against veranda poles and support columns, people begging, people talking, and people eating. Some were very well-dressed, some were dressed in work clothes, and some were barely dressed. But all were Zambian and all, it seemed, were looking at us. We walked past the crowd in front of the bank entrance and into the bank trying not to appear scared to death (we were), trying not to stare back at all the people staring at us (we didn't), trying not to stare at the two security guys in the bank with AK-47s (we did), and hoping we could exchange the money quickly and safely and get back on that bus (if it showed up).

We had to wait in line behind two Zambians. After they made their transactions, we stepped up to the counter. The teller, a very sharp looking Zambian woman with neatly done hair pulled into a jeweled comb, asked us what we needed in very clear Zambian-accented English. We said we would like to exchange our US dollars for Zambian currency. She did not look at the bag of cash, but rather kept her gaze fixed on us and asked for a passport. I gave her mine, she looked it over carefully and fully, looking from it to me and back to it several times. Seemingly convinced, she handed it back to me, opened the bag, and started counting it.

She said, "I count $3,000 US dollars?"

I hadn't thought to ask Brian how much was in there, nor did I count it, but I immediately replied, "Yes, that is correct, thank you." She then began writing out a receipt in typical African detail—literally about ten full minutes—during which time Cristi and I stood at full attention at her window, not daring to move, fidget, talk, or look around. When she began putting Zambian bills through an automatic counting machine, I shot Cristi a quick look of relief and confidence. But when the stacks kept coming, and coming, I began to wonder if the machine would be able to handle so many. Fifteen minutes later, we had a mountain of Zambian bills totaling 14.4 million *kwacha*, which in volume, would be the equivalent of $14 million US dollars in stacks of $100 bills. It would not have fit in a standard briefcase. Unconcerned and unimpressed, the teller pushed the money toward us and said, "Here is your money and receipt." Cristi and I blinked at each other. *What were we going to do with no backpack, no bags, no jackets, and no friends in this market place full of people who definitely could use some cash and at least two of them brandishing semi-automatic weapons?*

Without saying a word to each other, we put as much as we could back in the plastic bag and then stuffed the rest in every pocket of our cargo shorts and down our shirts. We walked out of there looking a bit like the kid in *A Christmas Story* when his mom suits him up for the cold and feeling a bit like Butch Cassidy and the Sundance Kid in their final scene. As we exited the bank to head into what felt like an arena, I whispered to Cristi out of the side of my mouth like a bad ventriloquist, "I guess we just smile and pray?" Without saying another word to each other, we used our couple's ESP and decided together that smiling was better than trying to look tough, so we smiled our way across the market to the spot where Brian dropped us off—hoping for a miracle. *How long would it take them to get a new passport? How long would it take them to get back? Should we just start handing out money to everyone in the market right now?*

We made it to the pick-up spot—still smiling—and looked around. No one in the marketplace had lost interest in us, in fact it seemed to be growing rapidly based on the number of people inching toward us. A Zambian man appeared from the crowd and came straight at us, half dancing and half stumbling, alternating between talking and singing. We could not understand a word he was saying and it quickly became apparent that it was not a language barrier—he was drunk. Liquor reeked from him as he approached me, not stopping until he stood toe-to-toe with me. I clutched the bag of money firmly, holding it down at my side, while he began poking me all over, singing a slurred song. Though the crowd seemed to have little respect for him, I felt sure they would have sided with him rather than us if we made a wrong move. Besides, they seemed to be entertained by what was happening. As they pointed and jeered, I began to wonder if this was another part of an elaborate setup. *Was this man just playing a part in a grand scheme to get us to react and retaliate so that the crowd could defend their countryman and justifiably take our money?* As this last thought raced to the forefront of my mind, it appeared that it was going to be true—the crowd literally parted like the Red Sea and I saw a very large, very fit Zambian man walking purposefully towards us with a severe scowl on his face, veins popping, eyes wide, and the unmistakable look of "justice is about to be served" throughout his whole body. "We are going to die," I whispered to Cristi as the smile quickly turned to a grimace, wondering if our families would get our bodies back.

It didn't take long for the Zambian hulk to reach us and as soon as he did he raised a massive right hand attached to a chiseled forearm and bulging biceps and quickly brought it down with a fury, and then, this is where a situation like this goes into ultra-slow motion, I will never forget the feeling that coursed through my entire body as the Zambian hulk's massive arm of justice hit its mark.

As his hand grabbed the town drunk by the back of the neck, he lifted him a good six inches off the ground and pulled him swiftly away from us. After taking two giant strides away, our Zambian hero looked back at us and said, "Sorry for your trouble." Then he carried the drunken man out of sight.

Still staring in disbelief and overwhelmed with relief, amazement, and gratitude (to God and the Zambian hulk), we came to our senses enough to see the Red Sea part again—this time a bit wider—as our bus pulled up with Brian hanging out the window. "Hey, you guys ready to go yet?"

Our driver—a local—must have accurately and quickly assessed the situation by the looks on our faces and the scene around us, because he barely, if at all, stopped the bus as we boarded, and then stomped on the gas pedal to take Butch and Sundance away. As we fell back into our bus seat, exhausted, relieved, and definitely ready to get out of there and head to the village, Brian, completely unfazed (and seemingly unimpressed as well), said, "Did you guys exchange the money?"

I said, "Yeah, all $14.4 million of it, dude!"

He said, "Okay, just hold on to it for now."

Really? That's it? Yeah, that's it—this was the developing world and we needed to get on board or figure out another "altruistic way to see the world" because this is how it works and if you can't take it all in stride, maintain perspective, and move on to the next challenge, then you aren't cut out for this work. That sunk in right then and there—*I got it, I can do this*—*here we go.* I had no idea that it was also about to change my life forever, that it was "here we go" for good.

Surely, the worst was behind us, right? We were all alive, we all had passports now, and we had $14.4 million dollars—well, $14 million in *kwacha*, but you get the point. With all that behind us, the beat-up-no-AC-bench-seats old bus seemed pretty good, and the two flat tires we got en route really didn't faze anyone. The bus was hot and we had to have all the windows down so we didn't roast to death, which made it a very, very dusty ride. But, we all still had the adventurer's spirit flowing strong in us as we shared the snacks we had brought, shared our music, and shared our stories—mostly the stories of this adventure that we had already experienced—the airport, the safari robbery, the embassy, the Zambian hulk. It turned out to be a ten-hour ride, so we even delved into childhood stories, and then childhood travel games, riddles, and songs. Bennie and Derek helped the bus driver change the tire, both times, and we stopped at three or four gas stations with small shops attached and less-than-ideal roadside toilets. It was intriguing to us that in each of these shops, as well as those in the airport and the market, there would be old televisions that all of the workers and customers were enraptured in watching. They seemingly were always on and I think they only got one channel. I am not sure where the feed came from, who chose it, or how shows made the cut, but we saw a cycle of the same shows that included BBC news, an African soap opera, football (soccer), and American WWF wrestling from the Hulk Hogan, Andre the Giant, and Macho Man era.

After each stop, we would get back on the road and Brian would patiently answer everyone's questions about what to expect, what we would do, what we would eat, and when we would get there. Bottom line, he didn't know the answers to any of the questions, but Brian has a great way of saying "I don't know" that makes you feel like that is a really good thing and there is no reason to worry.

While some people in the front of the bus finally started to nod off, I noticed from my seat in the back that the driver said something to Brian. Brian turned and announced that we were entering the village. We arrived in the village about 10:30 p.m. to the shouts of "*Mzungu! Mzungu!*" (white people) and literally at least a hundred kids joining the chase of the bus for the last half mile. We weren't sure if the chase and the shouting meant "You are rock stars, we love you, welcome to our village!" or "What do you stupid white people think you are doing in our village? If you stop this bus, we are going to kill you!"

The bus stopped in between two small, red clay brick Habitat houses at the edge of the village. In the darkness, it was hard to make out much detail, but we could see that to the front left of the bus was a giant dirt termite mound—taller than the bus—and surrounding the bus were all the kids and a very confused and sleepy looking older Zambian woman in her housecoat. Brian told us to stay on the bus, which no one argued with at this point, as he disembarked with his reassuring confidence and zest for adventure.

The good news was that it looked like the rock star sentiment was the one in play based on the kids smiling, singing, shouting, and engulfing Brian as he talked to the older woman. The bad news was that the conversation took longer than we felt it should, and when Brian got back on the bus it was with a combination of confusion and embarrassment to tell us that evidently Habitat had sent us to the wrong village and that they were not prepared to provide lodging, food, water, or work for us as they were not expecting a team at this site at this time.

Uh, what?

So much for being rock stars. *What were we going to do now?*

Brian informed us that the woman, Ms. Jean, said that there were two half-finished Habitat homes that the team could stay in for the night until we figured out what to do. Thankfully, the team was still at one hundred on the spirit-of-adventure scale. So, we jumped off the bus to more smiling, singing, shouting, and engulfing kids such that it felt like we crowd-surfed through the pitch-dark night to the houses we were to stay in.

Brian flipped on a headlight and a couple others on the team turned on flashlights to check out our accommodations. Half-finished was generous. The structures had no roofs, doors or glass in the windows, but further exploration showed that they did have plenty of giant spiders, mosquitoes, and bugs of unrecognizable species. It was hot outside and hotter inside. Still determined to make this work, the team took our bags from the kids who had joyfully unloaded them from the bus. We put them in the houses and asked where we could clean up and use the restroom before bed.

The kids crowd-surfed about half of us to the opposite end of the village to a row of almost-completed pit toilets while the other half of the team unpacked. These pit toilets made the roadside toilets look—and smell—like royal rose gardens. And, it being pitch dark in the wrong village certainly didn't help. This was the unmistakable moment on this project when some would say "the poop hit the fan." No pun intended.

Canadian Carrie lost it—she started pacing back and forth saying, "I can't do this, Brian, I can't do this! I just cannot do this!" Then I heard Toby and Sam both screaming about the spiders in their room and asking me to come help. *Why me? I guess because I am the vet?* Brian and Cristi went over to calm Carrie down while I went to kill spiders and everyone else stood around in apparent shock.

On my way back to the houses to kill as many spiders as I could, I noticed three things:

First, all the kids were gone and I remember wondering whether that was due to bed time, us going to the toilet area, or the team freak outs. I also noticed that Ms. Jean was walking hurriedly toward Brian and the team. And, I noticed Bennie, sitting on the termite mound, calmly and carefully taking stock of the whole situation. I could tell that he had gone into "protection mode" and had found the best vantage point to watch the team, cover all the exits, and jump into action wherever he was needed most, if it got to that. What I would come to learn was that—if you were "his people," which we had already unknowingly become—Bennie would do anything to care for you and keep you safe.

We would all also come to learn that Ms. Jean was one of the most caring, kind-hearted, and giving people that God ever put on this earth—she was one of my most profound and enduring glimpses at the beautiful faces and hearts of poverty—so it was no surprise that in taking in our situation and seeing the increasing anxiety from the team, she offered to open up her own home to the women on our team so that they could stay in a fully completed, furnished, safe and welcoming place. And I am sure she would have taken everyone in, but there was not nearly enough room in her humble home for us all.

Brian quickly sorted it all out with her while I was killing spiders with one of Cristi's tennis shoes as Toby and Sam took turns spotlighting each potential victim with their flashlight, each time saying, "There,

Jimi, there!" until we got to the giant one at the top corner of the room, at which time, Sam yelled, "Oh, Jimi, it's the mother, Jimi, the mother! Please get it, Jimi, it's the mother!" Which, honestly, still sounded so polite and polished with the British accent that I felt I was truly doing something ordained and heroic. Fortunately, I was able to exterminate "the mother" and even more impressively, that seemed to completely calm all their fears, such that we joined the team outside of Ms. Jean's house to formalize the plans for the night.

All the women, except for Cristi and Sam, would sleep at Ms. Jean's. Cristi and I, Sam and Toby, and the other men—Arizona husband, Derek, Bennie, and Brian—would stay in the half-finished houses.

It was past midnight at this point and we were travel-weary and exhausted. Yet still, we didn't sleep a wink. It was hot, unsettling, scary, and weird. Cristi and I shared her sleeping bag—mine was in my checked bag—and we tried to share her travel pillow—I didn't bring one. We put the sleeping bag down on the dirt floor, unzipped and unfolded, and laid on top of it, swatting mosquitoes and watching for giant bugs of unknown type. It was too hot to be too close together, and there was not much conversation, aside from this every thirty to forty-five minutes:

"You asleep?"

"No."

"You okay?"

"Yeah, I guess. Are you?"

"Yeah."

We didn't hear anyone else sleeping or snoring or screaming. I guess we were all "okay."

Morning did not come quickly. When we got up and walked out of our room at sunup, Brian was already sitting on one of four wooden benches that had been arranged in a square in the center of the village. On his bench, were three of the smaller kids we saw last night and on each of the other three benches were one or two adult male Zambians. They looked to be between forty and sixty years of age, dressed in hand-me-down clothes, drinking something from tin cups.

"Good morning!" Brian shouted as soon as he saw us. "Breakfast is almost ready!"

Brian has an amazing way of saying a lot in just a few words, staying positive in any situation, and making you feel like everything is completely under control, even when it's not. This approach definitely formed many of my developing-world situational management and leadership skills and strategies that have served me well to this day. The really good news was, that this time, everything really was under control again.

Brian talking with kids from the "wrong village" in Zambia

Apparently, sometime during the period of our tossing and turning and sweating in our open-sky rooms, the village had gotten the word out about our predicament, rallied the community and made a plan for us to stay. As the others came out of their rooms, and gathered around the benches, Brian introduced us to the men on the benches—and the kids—and then quickly got us all up to speed.

Ms. Jean and two of the other local women offered to get food and cook for us for every meal every day—it started with the breakfast Brian was referring to that morning and continued on through the entire ten days in the village. The village elders—the men on the benches that morning—would organize the community for the project. They would also take turns staying up all night around a campfire by where we were sleeping to ensure our safety.

Wait a minute—we are staying here? In the "wrong" village? Yes, the two Habitat team liaisons at the village we were supposed to be in got word to the village we were actually sent to right away to make sure we were safe—*and* could do our work there. The village we were in was a Habitat community too, and was approved for more homes, so—although it was no small undertaking—it just meant we had to shift plans and supplies and it could all be worked out. Besides, we had everything we needed: $14 million in cash, Brian, and Ms. Jean.

We worked in 100°F-plus temperatures every day, all day, hand-mixing cement and mortar, and hand-pressing and laying bricks. It was hard. It was exhausting. It was fun. It was exactly like we imagined. It was completely different than we imagined. It was way more than we imagined. When the work day was done, we took our solar shower bags and cleaned up the best we could. With my very limited wardrobe, I also had to do laundry almost every night, so I learned to combine that process by first showering with my clothes on while I also washed another T-shirt and underwear, and then slowly peeled off my work clothes, rinsed them and put them on the line as they went through my "MacGyvered" laundry cycle.

When we all got cleaned up the best we could, we would rotate through Ms. Jean's tiny house to get whatever delicacy she had prepared for us that day. There were always beans and rice and greens and then bread or maize or crackers to fill us up. About every third day, we got Ms. Jean's fried chicken. It truly was amazing! I am not kidding you, the colonel would be jealous. And, it is amazing how comforting, restoring, and calming food can be. That fried chicken, those meals, those conversations got us through and are lifetime memories for sure.

After dinner, we played soccer, played games, drew pictures, taught lessons, sang songs, and laughed with the amazing, beautiful, goofy, and strong kids from the village. I can't remember a time when we were there that we did not see smiles on their faces. And, as I would be "frozen" during a game of freeze tag, playing goalie in soccer, or bending-over-hands-on-knees to catch my breath, it would hit me like a ton of bricks—they have *nothing* in our terms—no shoes, one set of clothes, one meal a day—they are orphans. And yet, they are teaching me about joy. They are teaching me about being grateful and satisfied with what you do have, not focused on what you don't have. They are teaching me about the power of community, the power of working together for a shared future, the power of hope.

After play time, most of the team would head off to bed. But Brian, Bennie and I started hanging around the fire the second night we were there, and very quickly one of the elders, Daniel, gave us a head nod and patted the bench next to him, signaling to us that we were welcome to join the "council." This became my favorite ritual on that trip and still is to this day whenever we get that opportunity on our builds. It reminds me of the hundreds of wonderful hours I spent with my grandparents listening to their stories and learning about life. In the villages, it means that you are accepted, truly welcome, and considered family.

Daniel was a gentle, humble Zambian man in his early sixties (very old for this part of the world). He had been through tribal conflicts, famine and drought, malaria, and HIV epidemics, and had lived his whole life in poverty. He had seen pretty much every type of aid and charity come and go. He was not impressed with most, but he was with Habitat.

On our last night in the village, after two life-changing weeks of working shoulder-to-shoulder with this amazing community to build two homes with them and sharing many meals, many laughs, and many hugs, Daniel and I sat side-by-side by the fire and talked for hours. He told me about his struggles, the people he had seen die, the increasing number of orphans, the lack of educational opportunities, his dreams for his children, and his thoughts of how the community could solve these problems. He never once said they wanted money or expected others to solve these problems for them. He passionately talked about his faith—in God, in the community, in his family. He told me how proud he was of his kids—how smart they were and how well they were doing in school—he firmly believed that education was the key to their futures and the whole community's and country's future. He said they needed to focus on improving the schools to solve their problems.

His words and passion pierced me to my core. Earlier that day, my question to the kids had been asked and answered—"Books! Tuition!" The kids knew it, the parents knew it—*why didn't I know it? Why didn't the world know it?*

Then, I could see him take a deep breath, steel his nerves, look me dead in the eyes as if peering into my soul, and say to me, "Could I ask you a question?"

"Of course," I said.

Slowly, intently, and very purposefully he asked, "Why did you really come here?"

His question in that setting and asked in that way immediately put me in one of those out-of-body experiences where your thoughts become a rapid-fire series of movie scenes of your life that you are examining, like a lawyer questioning a defendant. *Why did I come here? Really? An altruistic way to see the world? A romanticized notion about saving the world? Guilt? Adventure? The next challenge?*

I honestly don't know how long I took to respond, but I do know that at some point the movie scenes stopped abruptly on the one of me at my veterinary school graduation where the photographer was taking a picture of my whole family with me. That's it—that is why I really came.

I looked at Daniel and said, "Daniel, I came because I have been blessed with the opportunities for an amazing education and the love, support, and encouragement needed to pursue all my dreams. I believe that every boy and girl deserves those same things and that God wants me to do everything in my power to help as many as I can in my lifetime—I know now that's why I came. And I am so glad I did."

He gave a single nod of his head and a guttural "Mmm," still locked in on my eyes as the window to my soul, then he gave me a slight shoulder bump as if to say, "That's a good reason" as he turned his gaze to the fire.

There was a long pause during which we both sat contemplating the conversation, the world, and life.

And then, Daniel finally broke the existential silence, and in the same profound manner as he asked the first question, he said, "I have to ask you one more question, please." With another deep breath, steeling of his nerves, and sincere anticipation of my answer, he asked, "That wrestling on the television, is it real?"

I smiled as his question once again put the perfect frame of perspective around the whole experience. "No," I replied, "it's just for entertainment."

He said thoughtfully and seriously, "I thought so."

The wrestling on television might not be real, but this experience in the "wrong" village sure was, and many lives were about to change—mostly mine.

RWANDA

There is something beautiful about having the chance to rewrite your future.
— CRYSTAL GENTILELLO

Irene is seventeen years old and in the second grade at the Butare Catholic de Primaire School in Rwanda. He is an orphan who lives on the street. He is a young man whose whole family was gunned down because they were from a "different tribe" than their killers. The hatred, the bloodlust, the passion to eradicate them was so intense—approximately one million people killed in one hundred days—that it must have spawned from deeply-held tribal differences and disputes between two very different groups of people in this small country, *right?*

Nope. The "differences" were contrived and created by outsiders— invaders and colonizers who used the oldest trick in the book— divide and conquer—to create internal battles among a once unified people to get, and keep, control and power. The plan worked. They gave special privileges to the Rwandans who were lighter-skinned, taller, and had thinner noses (who they dubbed the Tutsis) and helped them oppress the shorter, darker, broader-nosed Hutus to create class distinction that lead to division that lead to jealousy that lead to hatred, violence, and genocide.

This genocide was so cleverly designed and orchestrated that to the outside world, it was just crazed tribal in-fighting that we should let them sort out in their own violent tribal way and not get involved— and that is exactly what we did. We turned a blind eye to a brutal massacre. We let women be raped, mutilated, and then tortured to death. We let babies be slaughtered and thrown to the dogs. We let children be forced to kill their parents at gunpoint, and we slept at night in our warm beds in our comfortable homes knowing that it was just a bunch of crazy African tribal fighting that had nothing to do with us and nothing we could do anything about. We stood by despite begging and pleading from General Roméo Dallaire to intervene, despite pictures from journalists showing thousands of bodies piled in mass graves in the streets and ditches of every city, town, and village in Rwanda, and despite outcries from on-ground non-governmental organizations (NGOs) trying to stop the madness and save anyone they could.

General Dallaire said later that "the Rwandan story is the story of the failure of humanity to heed a call for help from an endangered people...we failed to move beyond self-interest for the sake of Rwanda...and to prevent the tragedy." He went on to say that, "The people of Rwanda were...individuals like myself, like my family, with every right and expectation of any human who is a member of our tortured race." This failure and neglect created hundreds of thousands of "Irenes" while much of the world did nothing other than shake our heads at how savage, ignorant, and mad African tribes can be. Oh, I forgot, we did do something—we apologized twenty years later. New Zealand ambassador Colin Keating addressed an open session of the United Nations Security Council in April of 2014 and said, "The genocide against the Tutsi highlighted the extent to which the UN methods of prevention utterly failed." I hope we never have to make another apology like that again.

When we met Irene, he was living on the street with no income, no family, no shoes and no opportunity. He was seventeen years old, but had lost ten years of his life due to the genocide. In the immediate aftermath, schooling was a low priority in terms of surviving, recovering, and healing. His school was still in shambles—the roofs were caved in or missing, the windows were all smashed out, the doors were off the hinges, and the walls all still had bullet holes in them. The bullet holes were right at chest level: the chest level of children—a constant reminder of the horror that occurred in schools all over the country—places of supposed safety, of learning, of a future. Add to that the embarrassment of only being at a second-grade level at seventeen years of age and I would dare to say that no one I know would ever even show up for one day at that place, much less go to school there. But Irene did. Every morning he got up, cleaned himself up the best he could, rolled up the blanket he used as a bed, and walked from whatever spot he found to sleep that night and went to school—to learn, to find a future, to find hope and to heal.

The headmaster and headmistress and the teachers there knew his story and they cared about him. Sometimes they let him sleep on the school grounds, even though it was against school rules. They brought him food when they could and they encouraged him to keep going in school, to complete his education so that he could get a good job and eventually have a place to live and a way to support himself.

This takes us back to Zambia. About a week into that trip, Brian starting telling us about three women he met through Habitat who were from Rwanda: Beata, Immaculee, and Margaret. These three Rwandan women had an incredible, heart-wrenching story of survival and resilience, having escaped the genocide, making it to the US, completing post-graduate degrees, and starting families in the eastern US. They completed the Habitat process for their own homes, which is how they got connected with Brian and became dear friends with him. Imagine the devastation of having everything and everyone you know and love taken away from you due to a genocide in your home country. Yet they each had the strength and courage, the education, and the hope for a better future to find a way to rebuild a life, build a career, and raise a family.

But they all still had one big dream in mind that they told Brian about one day.

"We want to rebuild our primary school!"

They credited their education, and especially their primary education with giving them the foundation, the inspiration, and the vision to fulfill their dreams. Ironically, that school was one of the many where Tutsis were brought to, under the guise of safety, and mass murdered during the genocide. It remained in shambles since that day. Beata, Immaculee, and Margaret felt that rebuilding this school and restoring it to a haven of inspiration and hope would physically and symbolically help rebuild the country, its people, and their dreams.

Even though it was not their intent in telling this to Brian, he took it on as a personal mission. He initially thought he could do it as a Habitat project, but soon realized that Habitat focuses on homes and not schools. Well, that only stopped Brian for about a millisecond. *No problem*, he thought, *I will just get a bunch of friends together who I know will buy into this and we will make it happen. We will do this one special school project and then I will go back to Habitat—business as usual.*

So, one night at the team dinner at Ms. Jean's, Brian told this story and asked the Zambian team if anyone was interested. Before the words were fully out of his mouth, Cristi said, "I'm in!" She was supposed to go to Rwanda in 1993 as part of her veterinary school graduation trip, but that leg of the trip was canceled because of the unstable and dangerous conditions in the country at that time—because of that, she followed the situation there and developed a heart for the people of Rwanda.

What was in my mind was, *Umm, could we talk about this please?* But I knew trying to change her mind would be futile and I loved that she was so passionate about it. What came out of my mouth was, "I would love to, but I don't think I can get that much time off work again so soon." (I am a recovering workaholic and I just could not see another two weeks away, completely off the grid, in less than ten months, happening for me.) But, what was burning in my heart was, *Dude, this is something you have to do, this is your purpose, this is something that will change lives, especially yours.*

By the end of the Zambia trip, my heart won and I was all in—we were going to Rwanda for a one-time school build as our next altruistic way to see the world. It will be cool, Cristi will be happy, and then we can take a break for a while—business as usual.

But, then we went to Beata's, Immaculee's, and Margaret's—and Irene's school in Rwanda.

I will never forget walking up to that school in the late afternoon on the day we arrived. We entered through the main gate, which was pulled mostly off its hinges, twisted, and bent. As we passed the main administration building, which looked abandoned, we walked through the assembly yard between buildings. As we kept going further inside the campus, an eerie feeling came over me, and Cristi verbalized it.

"So much bad has happened here, it is overwhelming."

"Yeah," was all I could say.

We passed what was once the library—broken out windows, battered doors, faded paint. We entered the big school yard and then saw the classrooms that we were there to rebuild. To me, it looked like the bunkers you see in the old war movies. Roof caved in, windows shattered, doors and door frames broken and falling down. And, then we stepped inside.

I couldn't breathe. I couldn't wrap my head around it.

I couldn't hold back the tears.

The team of thirty people stood in silence, disbelief, and confusion.

What were all the holes in the wall? How could a school look like this? What happened here?

Again, Cristi verbalized what we were all seeing. I think she had to say it in order for us to be able to acknowledge it and move forward.

"Those are bullet holes."

All around the classroom walls. In the chalkboards. In all four of the classrooms. Bullet holes, everywhere.

I am glad it was late afternoon and day one was just for the tour and planning. I could not have worked that day. Even Brian was at a loss for words and could not find his usual "don't worry, everything will be fine" face.

We went back to the hotel, picked at dinner, and turned in early. We all had to process what we saw, what had happened in this place, and what we were going to do about it.

The next day, we met Irene, Beata, Margaret (Immaculee could not make this trip) and so many more amazing Rwandans. Students, parents, grandparents, former students and community members came out to work on the school every day, and work hard! They came to reclaim their school. The came to rebuild their school. They came to rewrite their future.

Three images of the work capture it all for me and will forever remain in my mind and heart.

The first is of Irene taking one of our team members, Glenn, by the hand to lead him to one of the classroom windows that was broken and detached, swinging and creaking in the wind. Irene is a seventeen-year-old Rwandan who speaks only the Kinyarwandan language. Glenn is a seventy-eight-year-old American who speaks only the English language. But they immediately "spoke" the same language of school building. Together, they ripped out the old window, cleaned up the opening, measured for the new one, and started rebuilding it. Pointing, saying the relevant word in their own language, demonstrating, charades, and lots of laughter got the job done. On the outside, they could not be more different. On the inside, they shared the exact same mission and goal—they would not let darkness remain, they would not let hate win—they would restore this school, restore the opportunity for education, restore safety... restore hope.

The second image is of Cristi, Mo, Hannah (yep, same two from Zambia), Loretta, Diana, Jacquie and Dominique (Brian's wife) spread completely across a wall-length chalkboard—seven white women—interspersed every other one with five black Rwandan students and one black Rwandan teacher filling in the bullet holes in that wall. Not many words were spoken as I watched, but so many things were said by what they were doing. Each one had their bucket of plaster and putty knife. Each one took great care to completely fill in each hole. Together, they filled the holes in the wall, which filled the holes in their hearts and minds—not erasing what had happened, but signifying that things could be restored and they could move forward in education, in opportunity...in hope.

The third is of one of our team members, Jimmy, from Louisiana. Jimmy was "just a good ol' boy contractor" born and raised on Cajun cooking, hard work, and southern hospitality. He did not have a lot growing up and he lost a lot when Hurricane Katrina hit. He had also suffered a great loss in recently losing his wife to cancer. But all he wanted to do was help others. Being the only construction professional we had on the build, Jimmy got the roofing job, which was a big job. He recruited and coached the older students and some brave and dedicated parents to completely redo the destroyed roof that spanned all four classrooms. The image that said it all was the one of Jimmy right after he helped one of the parents put the last nail in the ridge cap to finish off the project, and then turned around, sat down, and gathered his whole roofing team around him for a picture. He hollered down at me to take a picture and when I looked up, all I could do was grin from ear to ear. There was Jimmy, the Cajun contractor, sitting on the top of this beautiful new roof in Butare, Rwanda, completely surrounded by his team of Rwandan students and parents—all of them beaming with satisfaction, pride, and connection. Together, they took a completely destroyed roof and restored it completely. I started to say, "Smile for the picture," but there was no need. They were smiling, laughing, posing, and glowing...with hope.

After ten days of hard work together as Rwandans, Americans, South Africans, and Germans—as *people*—that school was transformed from a broken bunker of tragedy, heartache, and despair into a completely restored, safe, and inviting block of four classrooms with bright green doors and windows and a shiny new roof. The rooms featured freshly painted blackboards and were filled with beautifully varnished desks, wall maps, window stickers, chalk, and books—and no bullet holes.

It was time to celebrate, and celebrate we did! The festivities were all set up in the school yard against the backdrop of the new classrooms. There was wonderful traditional Rwandan music and dancing. There were speeches. There were gifts. There were more speeches. There was more music and dancing. Beata and Margaret, dressed in colorful, traditional Rwandan ceremonial *mushanana* dresses and headdresses, walked over to the main classroom door, followed closely by the whole crowd, and paused, taking many long, deep and thoughtful breaths. And together, with tears rolling down their cheeks, they cut the ribbon and declared this school open for learning! *That*, my friends is what it is all about. That is their dream come true! That is the promise kept to kids who wanted *Books!* and *Tuition!* That is *being the change*!

One of the restored classrooms in Rwanda full of excited students and an engaged teacher

After the celebration and dedication, Cristi, Dominique, Brian, and I were sitting with a group of local leaders—men and women, tall and short, dark and light skinned—and two poignant conversations occurred that shaped my perspective from that day forward. After working side by side with the amazing people of Butare and feeling comfortable with the friendships forged and their willingness, and in fact need, to talk about the genocide, we respectfully asked those in this group if they were Tutsi or Hutu. I will never forget the answer that immediately came from the lips of every single person we asked. With their heads held high and a strength in their voice and passion from their souls, each would say "I am Rwandan!"

Yes, and they always were—if only we would have let them be Rwandan, how different would things be?

And, then, without thinking about it or rehearsing it, I just said "I'm sorry we did not do more! I'm sorry we did not help stop the genocide!" After a very short silence that was serene and heavy, but not at all uncomfortable, a very old and wise woman captured me in a locked-in gaze like a hypnotist achieving her trance, and said "We cannot retread our bloody steps and wipe them clean, but we can widen and smooth the path leading to our future. You have made the path broader and easier for our children and for that we are forever grateful."

I only had emotions—no words—and just stood, went to her, and embraced her for a brief moment and then went to my room to pack. *Could school building really do that? Can we help change the world, change children's futures for the better, by spending two weeks helping a community rebuild a school?* In her words, I knew beyond a shadow of a doubt that the answer was *yes* and I knew beyond a shadow of a doubt that we had to keep on being path smoothers and wideners for "crazy tribal madmen" like these beautiful amazing Rwandans wherever we could for as long as we could.

This was all burning inside me as Cristi and I packed and I could physically feel it build to the point of eruption—it was powerful—but it was not emotional, it was clear and certain. Holding a sock in one hand and a T-shirt in the other, I turned to Cristi and said, "I know what we have to do."

Still packing and only half listening, she replied, "What's that?"

"We have to build schools."

"We just built a school, sweetie."

"No, we have to build schools our whole lives."

She stopped packing. She looked at me carefully and thoughtfully to see if I was just messing with her as I so often like to do or if this was serious. It was clear that I was very serious. And, it immediately became a shared moment of clarity of what we "had to do." We had to build schools our whole lives—we had to help improve educational opportunities for boys and girls, men and women, we had to get kids books and tuition, we had to use the most powerful weapon for change to help people realize their dreams, we had to hand deliver hope.

Her confirmation and commitment came out in three simple words.

"Yep, you're right."

When we delivered this news to Brian (and Dominique, his South African wife—another story for another book), he said, "Okay, let's do it."

So, *Be The Change Volunteers* was born. The seed came from orphans in Zambia, the germination happened in the genocide-rubble of Rwanda, the sprouting happened in Columbia, Missouri, and the rest of this book is about our growth into a strong tree with many branches that stretch across the globe.

What about Irene, you ask? Irene worked so hard for two straight weeks rebuilding *his* school, painting *his* school, cleaning *his* school. He and I talked—lots of trying to understand each other's language and accents, lots of sign language, lots of puzzled looks, lots of laughing—we worked together, played together, and just spent time together. I asked him what his dream was, and he said, "A good job and a family...and a home." I asked Beata how we could help him with that—in the right way. She said, "Books! Tuition!" So, Cristi and I talked and decided to sponsor Irene for his educational needs.

This was the start of what would eventually become our *BTCV Kids* program, and has yielded more return on investment than we could've imagined. In the years since this first BTCV project, he completed grade eight, went to vocational school to train as a draftsman, got a job with a regional heavy construction company, and was able to rent a small house. And yep, he got married—and started a family. Hand delivered hope turned into dreams come true for a deserving young man who was willing to go back to grade two at the age of seventeen and use the power of education to make them come true. *Is there any better return on investment than that? See why we got hooked?*

CAMBODIA

It takes but one person, one moment, one conviction, to start a ripple of change.
—Donna Brazile

Imagine you are a Vietnamese person in Cambodia. You escaped the terror in your homeland to this neighboring country that has seen its own share of terror and you are trying to start over in this foreign land. They do not speak your language, you can live there, but you are not allowed to own land, so what do you do? Well, there is a very big lake in Cambodia. If you cannot own land, maybe you can live on the water—literally on the water. You make a house boat, really a shack boat, and you hook your shack boat up to other Vietnamese shack boats and start a floating village. You have to figure out and learn a new way to make money and fishing is pretty much the only reasonable choice for your floating village on Tonle Sap Lake, so you and your family become fishermen.

Now, what about the kids? Are they allowed to go to school there? Yes, excellent! But, wait—there are a few problems. First, you have to buy them uniforms and school supplies. Okay, you can figure that out—more fishing, a bit less food, and no fixing up the shack boat right now. Next, you have to get them to the school. *Where is the school?* Well, the one closest to your floating village is in Siem Reap. Sounds good, the kids can paddle the family canoe there—it's not too far. That way, you can keep fishing and make as much money as you can to support the family and the kids' education. This will work.

And it does, for about five to six months out of the year, during the rainy season when Tonle Sap Lake is at peak levels and your floating village is close to the school in Siem Reap. And then, the dry season comes, and Tonle Sap Lake levels decrease drastically and the lake contracts, and your floating village floats far away from Siem Reap and the school. The kids cannot readily get to the school by any reasonable means, so they don't go to school, so they get behind, until they quit, usually by grade two or three.

So, if Mohammed cannot go to the mountain, then the mountain must come to Mohammed (or something like that).

Next stop on the newly christened BTCV train—helping a community build a Floating Learning Center on Tonle Sap Lake. Nothing like jumping in with both feet, right? No one on the BTCV core team was a contractor, architect, or civil engineer—but what the heck, they needed a floating school, so we decided to help them build a floating school for our second project ever. And we did, by partnering with the local community. They had contractors, architects, and civil engineers, who were now fishermen and fisherwomen and wanted nothing more than to use their skills to help reshape their kids' futures. And they did it! The community did an incredible job pooling their resources and expertise, and with some support from BTCV and help from our team, the community constructed a beautiful Floating Learning Center. And, man, did they ever use it. They rotated the children through from early morning to evening to get all the grade levels taught and then did literacy and vocational training for the adults after dinner. If you (help) build it, they will come ... and keep coming to learn, to share, to grow, and to build the future for the community and their kids. It was such an incredible story that Tonle Sap Lake Floating Learning Center actually became one of the sites to see on at least one of the official Siem Reap tour routes.

To build this floating school, we took a boat to the work site on the lake each day. The boats were typically large, hand-crafted canoes with converted car engines in the middle and a long, direct shaft-to-propeller drive system—it was basically a drag boat canoe with one major difference. The crew had to frequently crank the propeller out of the water to clean off the thick weeds that got wrapped around it every half mile or so, as the weeds were very dense and thick in that lake. As soon as the captain felt the strain on the engine from the entangled weeds, he would stop the boat, and a crew member would crank up the shaft and clean the propeller. Then, they would crank it back down and off we would go again, until the next cleaning session.

I could definitely relate to the crew's job because my favorite summer job of all time was being the crew for my Grandpa Gordon. Grandpa always kept a current-model ski boat at their lake house in Indiana and would take all the kids and adults from the nearby lakefront homes waterskiing, tubing, and cruising pretty much non-stop throughout the summer. Living four houses down from him and idolizing him like the superhero he was, I was his boat crew. Like the weed crew in Cambodia, I would untangle ski ropes, adjust ski bindings, pick out the right life preserver, and relay the skiers signals about boat speed, route, and duration to Captain Grandpa. I loved those hours in the boat with the main father-figure in my life. It gave me time with my Grandpa whose extremely strong work ethic, heart for others, giving spirit, unimpeachable character, and rock-solid faith helped mold me, inspire me, and drive me. I am certain that I would not be involved in helping build a floating school on Tonle Sap Lake without those hours in the boat on Winona Lake with my grandpa.

Once we got out to the floating work site, we would stay the whole day so that we could complete the project—building it from floor joists on a boat hull to finished classrooms and teachers' quarters—in two weeks. They had lunch for us on the boat each day, and boy, were we ready for it each and every day. We worked hard and it was made even more mentally challenging because pretty much no one spoke each other's language. On the team, we had Americans, South Africans, a couple of Canadians, and a group from Hong Kong, while our local guides and aids were Cambodian, and the community members and kids were all Vietnamese. Talk about the Tower of Babel! But, we figured it out every day and got the job done well—with sign language, the telephone game, and the few words we picked up from each other. The only words I remember from that trip are *thuyen truong hoc*, which I was told means "boat school."

On the last day of work, we were working hard to get everything done for the big dedication and celebration the following day and I had just dipped up a plate of food and eased my way onto the floor with my muscles protesting silently but violently the whole way. I gulped down a long drink of water and was just bringing the first heaping fork full of fish and rice to my lips when I looked up to see Dominique standing over me.

"Jimi, a young boy has hurt his arm, would you be able to look at it please?" she said calmly and sweetly with her melodic South African accent.

I said, "Sure, I would be happy to," thinking by the way she said it that she meant this happened a while ago and that I could look at him at my convenience to provide advice about medical care he could seek.

So, I took that big bite of food and teed up another one. I looked back up and Dominique was still standing there, now with a confused look on her face. I raised my eyebrows in a friendly but I-already-answered-your-question kind of way, which prompted her to say, "Could you please look at him now? He is in a lot of pain." Realizing the urgency, I hopped up, grabbed our small first aid kit and Cristi, and followed Dominique to our boat, which took us to where the injured boy was—his uncle's house in the floating village.

On the way, our local guide and Dominique told me what happened. The boy, named Uk, who was an approximately thirteen-year-old Vietnamese boy, was helping his uncle fish from their boat. Besides helping with the nets, Uk's job was to clean weeds off the propeller when needed. Even at this young age, Uk had done this thousands of times without any problems. Well this time, Uk cleaned the propeller, cranked it down, and told his uncle it was okay to start the engine again. But then he saw some weeds he missed and reached down to remove them from the propeller, right when his uncle started the engine. The spinning propeller met wrist, in very contaminated water, on a lake in the developing world. Very bad combination.

We reached the uncle's shack boat and in my now hyper-aware state of concern for the boy and seeing the uncle waiting by the doorway with the unmistakable look of guilt-ridden pleading for help, I leapt onto the shack boat just as our boat pulled up. I headed into the house to where the uncle wordlessly directed me with a visibly shaking hand to the boy and eyes that said *please help my nephew*. The boy was on a bed in the front room of the shack boat, in the fetal position, face as white as a ghost, writhing and moaning very quietly. I knelt on the bed beside him to comfort him and assess the injury. It was bad. Grossly contaminated, bone protruding from the skin wound which was a propeller gash, very displaced and crooked. The good news was that it was fresh, he was young, and he had blood flow and feeling in his hand—could be worse.

Well, in a way it was worse, in my intense focus to get to the boy and help him, I committed a major cultural taboo. Not only did I enter the house without taking my shoes off, I was on their bed with my shoes on. This was bad, really bad. Probably similar to someone coming into your house and urinating on your living room carpet—seriously. I looked up to see where Cristi was with the first aid kit and saw three faces filled with the combination of horror and embarrassment—our local guide and Uk's aunt and uncle—and two faces filled with fear and urgency—Cristi's and Dominique's.

In her remarkable calm confident way, Cristi, who had taken her shoes off before entering the house, quickly came to the edge of the bed, smoothly slipped my shoes off and took them outside. Then, smiling at the aunt and uncle the whole way, she brought me the first aid kit and said, "What do you need first?" Realizing how she just orchestrated this incredible save, I just smiled at her, tried to look lovingly into her eyes, and said, "Thanks! I need the betadine scrub brushes please."

As we provided some first aid to this young boy, I asked our guide how to say "It's okay" in Vietnamese. Our guide, said *"Duoc Roi."* So, as I tried my best to pronounce it and sound reassuring to Uk, in my southern American accent (with my shoes off), we were able to get the wound cleaned up and the bones back in place.

Once we had the urgent first aid treatment accomplished, we needed to protect his arm so they could get him to some medical treatment, *but how?* We had no bandaging material in the first aid kit. Then, Cristi remembered we had just done the molding around the doors and that we had brought toilet paper out with us from the hotel, so after my first thought of *that's ridiculous*, I decided her idea could work and sent Cristi to fetch both while I continued to clean and then dry Uk's arm. Cristi returned with the "bandaging materials" and I put a toilet-paper-door-molding splint on Uk that was about as pretty as a warthog, but thankfully was functional for now. I told our guide to tell him to keep it very clean and dry until they could get it further treated. The message got delivered, and I now saw six smiling and relieved faces. As I put my shoes on and hopped in the boat while giving Uk one more "doo-ack raw," the color came back into his face and he actually forced out a smile.

When we came back the next day, I wanted to find Uk right away and make sure everything was taken care of so that I could help prepare for the celebration and enjoy this wonderful event with the community, who turned out in full force and regalia. But, I looked everywhere and asked everyone, and still could not find Uk. So I started working on the celebration preparations and visiting with the various community dignitaries who came for the event—then, out of the corner of my eye, I saw him. *Good, he's here, not septic, not lying in bed writhing in pain.* But, wait a minute, something was wrong—he seemed to be trying to hide and he did not look right. *What is going on?*

I headed over towards him and called his name, and as he ashamedly turned around, I saw why. The splint was gone. Something was wrapped around his wrist, and his hand was pointed sixty degrees the wrong way again.

"What happened? Uk, what happened?!"

Uk does not speak any English, so he just looked at me with those scared, sad, and painful eyes again. We finally got the telephone game of multilingual communication to work enough to find out that when Uk told his parents what happened and showed them the splint, they immediately took him to the floating village's witch doctor to get him treated in the traditional way. The witch doctor was happy to comply, for the requisite fee, and took the splint off immediately, blew into the wound, and then wrapped a bark and seaweed combination dressing around it to "heal it correctly." Shockingly, that did not work. The arm was crooked again, the wound now had bark and seaweed on it, and in it, and Uk was in pain and headed toward having a crooked, painful, non-functional dominant arm for the rest of his life.

Well, what was done was done. We just had to get it cleaned up again and make sure he got some proper treatment this time.

"Uk, come on over here."

Again, Uk does not speak any English, but that was not the problem now. He figured out my sign language and the look on my face. The problem now was that his parents were not going to allow any western medicine for him. *What were we going to do?* I could not leave this poor kid like this. I had to figure out a way to explain this to them, *but how?* I cannot speak a lick of Vietnamese or Khmer (Cambodian language) and charades weren't going to cut it for that situation. Back to the multilingual telephone game with our Cambodian guides, Vietnamese guides and Uk's parents and uncle. I truly have no idea what was said in the conversation, but they agreed to let me look at it at least. But, only under the very watchful eyes of the family, and a rapidly growing crowd of onlookers who wondered what black magic I was going to perform.

Cristi and I sat down with Uk on a bench and literally were completely closed in on by the onlookers. Pictures I saw later looked like the largest football huddle you can imagine composed of Cambodian and Vietnamese people of every age and size. I do remember that it was very hot in the eye of the huddle and I was a bit nervous. I took the bark and seaweed wrap off and assessed the situation. Fortunately, it was still pretty clean other than the bark residue and at least the bone was not sticking through the wound again. I grabbed another scrub brush and showed it to the parents and the crowd and pretended to scrub my own arm as a demonstration of what I was asking to do to Uk's arm. A wave of *mmms* and *oohs* went in and out and around the mega huddle and finally Uk's dad nodded okay. I started scrubbing Uk's arm again gently while Cristi started gathering the proper bandaging supplies we were able to find at a pharmacy in Siem Reap the previous night. I was still gently scrubbing Uk's arm and trying not to make it painful as I did not want Uk, his parents, or the onlookers to panic and throw us off the boat for practicing black magic that hurt their son.

I was working through the process of scrubbing, straightening, and looking up and smiling when all of a sudden there was another set of hands scrubbing his arm—pretty vigorously, I must say. I looked up to see what was going on and saw the face of a young girl sitting right next to me. I had no idea who she was, how she got there through the mega huddle, and why she was trying to help. And I did not know how I was going to deal with this new variable. So, in my best loud voice (because that always helps people interpret your language) with my best charades, I said and demonstrated, *"Careful! Broken! Arm Hurt! Gentle!"* In perfect English, she said, "I know, I am here to help you."

There was no time to ask, *where did you come from, where did you learn English, where have you been all week?* So I simply said, "Okay, thanks," and we got back to work. She held his arm, helped clean, and explained everything to the mega huddle in what I learned later was perfect Vietnamese and perfect Khmer. Together, we got Uk's arm cleaned up, fixed up, and bandaged again. As soon as we did, all the color came back to his face and he gave us a big smile.

The combination of Uk's response and Reachana's (the multilingual medical angel's name) narration and explanation convinced his parents and the mega huddle that this was all okay. Once the first aid cleaning and bandaging were complete, Uk stood up to show his father, who touched it cautiously, then felt Uk's fingers, then looked Uk in the eyes, and then smiled. A cheer went up from the mega huddle and Uk became the teen idol as he made his way through the crowd letting them touch, feel, and smell, *yes smell*, his bandaged arm. All was good, especially after Reachana translated our advice for getting a cast put on the arm as soon as possible and how that would "make his arm come right" so he could go back to doing all the things a thirteen-year-old Vietnamese boy should do.

Jimi, Reachana, Uk and Cristi after treating Uk's injury the second time

As we stood there for a brief moment taking in this extraordinary scene and experience, Brian and Dominique grabbed us and said, "It's time to start the dedication and celebration." Oh wow, I almost forgot about that. *Okay, let's go.*

The celebration was incredible—exquisite traditional music and dancing—so different from the Rwandan music and dancing and yet equally as artistic and moving. Then, there were heartfelt speeches from the floating village's mayor, police chief, Catholic priest, and students. Their words, when translated to us, spoke of unity, opportunity, the future, and hope—they seemed genuinely grateful and moved by our work with them, but they definitely understood it was *their* Floating Learning Center, it was blue*, and its success and sustainability were dependent on them.

I was sitting across from Reachana during the celebration and watched her most of the time. She was beaming, singing all the songs, and seemed to pour her entire spirit into every part of it. She listened to every speech—in all three languages—and nodded at important and impassioned points during each one. After the celebration was over and the pictures were taken and the hugs were exchanged, I immediately went to find her. I said, "Reachana, thank you again for your help today—you did a great job and I am very grateful! How did you learn to speak three languages so well?" She said simply, "School."

"How were you able to go so far in school and do so well?"

"I paddled boat to school when I could or I find transport with anyone who will take me."

I said, "Wow, you must really love school?"

She said, "I want to learn."

"That's awesome, what is your dream?"

"I want to go to nursing school, but it is impossible."

"Why is it impossible? Did you not qualify for nursing school or is there no school close by?"

"I qualified on the national exam and there is a good nursing school in Siem Reap."

"Why is it impossible then?"

"It requires too much money."

"How much is it?"

"It would be disrespectful to even tell you."

"Please just tell me how much it is, it is not disrespectful at all to me."

"Please sir, I cannot."

"Cristi, come over here and find out how much it is."

Cristi spoke with her woman-to-woman (calmly and encouragingly) not like Jimi the Interrogator. Finally, she told Cristi the amount: $2,500. *A semester?* No. *A year?* No. *Total?* Yes. *Are you kidding me? Done!* This is *BTCV Kid* number two for sure! A total of $2,500 to help a young girl living in Cambodia who figured out a way to keep going to school no matter what, learned three languages, scored high enough on the national exam to get into nursing school, and was able to educate a boy's skeptical family about how to get the best care for their son—this is the definition of a no-brainer!

We got her contact information and told her that we would provide the funding if she got everything done on her end. I am not sure she really believed it at that time. We told her we did need two favors from her though in return. 1) We needed her to make sure Uk and his family completed the care needed to get his arm healed, and 2) we needed her to do really well in nursing school and come back and help her floating village in the ways that she could when she graduated. She happily agreed to both.

We left Cambodia even more inspired and energized about school building. We were confident that we were on the right path and going about it the right way so far and that we could have a positive impact on the world this way—one student, one school, one village at a time.

About two months after we got home from Cambodia, we received an email from Reachana (Brian and Dominique had gotten her set up with email access through the hotel where we stayed in Siem Reap). There were just two short lines of text:

Uk arm is fine. Cast removed and arm very straight. He and family happy.

I am accepted nursing school. Can it really be?

And a picture was attached—of her standing next to Uk on the Floating Learning Center. Both his arms were extended in front of him to show how straight his arm had healed and how the wound had healed up well also. Both of them had beautiful big smiles on their faces, radiating joy—true joy.

We got Reachana all set up with funding for school. We got regular emails and irregular phone calls—always between 2:00 and 3:00 a.m. our time as she could never quite figure out the time difference—but as veterinarians we were used to dead-of-night phone calls. Reachana always began the calls with, "Daddy, or Mommy, is that you?" With that term of endearment and respect starting a call from an amazing young lady who was fighting all odds to learn, mature, and accomplish her big hairy audacious goal (BHAG) for her family and community, *how could we ever be the least bit upset?* And we never were.

We received these calls all throughout her schooling, which she did complete. And she did go back to her floating village to help them with their healthcare and their education. In fact, two pictures which I will keep forever and will always give me goosebumps are ones she sent me several years later.

One is of Uk, now a rather tall young man, handsome, with the same big smile on his face as in the cast-removal picture, but he has matured a lot. He looks strong as he stands in his own fishing boat holding (with two straight and strong arms) a big fishing net, poised to throw the net but willing to pause for a picture for his American first aid friends from years ago.

The other is of Reachana, sitting on the floor of the Floating Learning Center cross-legged, next to a tiny Vietnamese girl of about four or five years old. Reachana is tending to a small scrape on the little girl's arm. The little girl is sitting cross-legged too in her beautiful school uniform looking up at Reachana with an unmistakable look of awe-inspired hero-worship. The look says it all—*Reachana did it, now I know I can too!*

We went back to visit the Floating Learning Center and Reachana nine years later. Reachana lives and works in Siem Reap and hosted us for a site visit to check on the center and discuss the next phases of projects there. She now has a beautiful family of her own, including her husband and two daughters and another child on the way. Reachana regularly visits the Floating Learning Center, bringing supplies, working with them on hygiene and healthcare, and encouraging them to continue their educations in pursuit of their own dreams. She has also started her own local version of our *BTCV Kids* program by supporting three children from her village for their schooling. When we asked Reachana why she decided to help these children when she has her own to take care of with limited resources, she said, "Because we should not only see the world through our own eyes!"

I think this is working—*what do you think?*

In Cambodia, we learned one of the many important lessons we needed to learn in order to do development aid the right way—the lesson was about always doing things in a culturally appropriate way. In the developed world, especially the US, it seems we have lost or moved away from many of our cultural roots and traditions and place little focus or importance on them, which I think is very sad.

In the developing world, the cultural roots and traditions are still very strongly held, used, and valued, which is one of the many things I love about working with these communities. One of the cultural traditions in the floating community was the importance and symbolism of colors. For the floating communities, colors symbolized religious and cultural sects. If the school was red, the families of one sect would not send their kids there, if it was yellow, the families of another sect would not send their kids there, but blue meant "open to all"—so the Floating Learning Center is blue.

This really impressed upon us how important it is to 1) learn about the cultural roots, traditions, and taboos long before going into the community, 2) educate the team on how best to respect them, and 3) don't build American schools with American curriculum—build culturally appropriate schools and let the community drive the curriculum to what they need, accept, and can best use to reshape their futures. We are extremely glad to have learned this lesson early on and continue to carefully employ it for each project and community.

PAPUA NEW GUINEA

Travel is fatal to prejudice, bigotry, and narrow-mindedness, and many of our people need it sorely on these accounts. Broad, wholesome, charitable views of men and things cannot be acquired by vegetating in one little corner of the earth all one's lifetime.

—MARK TWAIN

Cannibals, head hunters, witch doctors, and sing-sings were all I really "knew" about Papua New Guinea (PNG), when Brian told me this would be a great spot for our next build. He said he built Habitat for Humanity homes there and had a great local contact in PNG named Martin. As an extremely goal-oriented person, I decided we needed a BHAG (Big Hairy Audacious Goal: credit to Jim Collins, author and consultant for business management and corporate sustainability and growth) for Be The Change Volunteers. I then decided that goal would be for BTCV to complete at least one hundred education-focused development aid projects before I died. To signify this goal, each project would get a three-digit number, so Rwanda was 001, Cambodia was 002, and now we needed 003. Brian, Dominique, and Cristi were on board with this and so we decided we needed to ramp up the projects if we were going to make it to one hundred before I died and that to do that, we needed to divide and conquer. So, Brian and Dominique would organize and lead some builds and Cristi and I would organize and lead other builds. Brian thought PNG would be a great place and that I would really like going there, so I said, "Let's do it. Give me Martin's contact info and I will get to work on it."

Now, PNG is a very, very, very long way away from the US, is very isolated from technology, and does have a bit of a reputation for danger and reluctance to accept outsiders, so this may not have been the best choice for my first project as organizer and leader. But because Martin truly is a remarkable individual and by the grace of God, we found our way through travel logistics, visa hurdles, and stereotypes and stigmas to build a team of ten brave volunteers, now known as *Changers*, raise funds to build a three-classroom building, and make our way across the world in sixty-three hours to arrive in Apangai, Papua New Guinea, and meet Martin in person.

And what an arrival it was. The welcoming ceremony was like something from *National Geographic's* greatest hits. Community members from the seven villages served by the school that we would be working on came out in full force, adorned in the most amazing grass skirts, floral aprons, headdresses, face paint, tattoos, and native shell, bone, and bead jewelry. They lined the path that we walked from the bus to the village center, adorning us with fresh-flower leis, cheering like we were the Beatles in their prime, and fanning us with giant palm leaves to keep us cool. There was music—amazing, tribal, rhythmic music. There were smiles—some gleaming white, some deeply red-stained from the betel nut, and some toothless—but all genuine and beautiful. We were escorted to the village center's covered platform and given fresh juice, more leis, and seated on the platform that bore a giant hand-painted sign welcoming us to Papua New Guinea. We felt very welcomed—and safe. There were speeches, dancing, singing—and more speeches, more dancing, more singing.

On the surface, you probably could not pick two more different groups of people than the ten white Americans on the team and the hundreds of black Papua New Guineans from the villages, but the shared purpose, open hearts, and genuine smiles made us instantly and completely alike. It was an amazing feeling that I now realize is the wonderful reality that humanity is supposed to be and that we all deeply crave whether we know it or not. This is an earth-shattering perspective-changer that volunteers on our teams are always exposed to—most of them "get it" and are forever changed for the better. Some don't, which is a great loss to them. I truly believe that if we could all "get this" and apply it to everyone in every place, we would experience a form of heaven on earth.

The community involvement certainly did not stop at the welcoming ceremony. We had more than a hundred students, teachers, parents, grandparents, and engaged community members on site each day working hard! This was a project where we literally went from the first shovel full of dirt for digging the foundation to three complete classrooms with students' desks, teachers' desks, new chalkboards, and freshly painted walls in nine days of work.

On the second day of work, we were hauling rocks from the river bed about 200 feet down the hill to bring up to the site for the foundation. It was a steep hill, the rocks were heavy, and we were using the traditional means of hauling them—in halved tree trunks on our shoulders. I take pride in never being outworked on a build, so I chose a very large trunk for my rock hauling. I had made about three or four trips and had made friends with a small boy of about five or six years of age who became my rock loader. He would wait for me by the river's edge, gathering "the best" rocks for me, and then helped me load them up in the tree trunk to haul up to the site. We quickly had a good system in place and we were having great fun comparing rocks, trying to load the trunk to the max without losing any rocks, skipping the "rejects" across the river, and making faces at each other. I was having a wonderful day—this is what I love to do on a build.

The rock hauling assembly line, consisting of dozens of community members and Changers, was continually going up and down the hill to bring in the massive amount of rock needed for the large foundation. I was pretty focused on my work and my interactions with my chief rock loader so did not recognize much else that was going on until my eighth or ninth trip up the hill. I was hauling my very large (single) tree trunk load of rocks up the hill when I noticed a woman pass me (quite easily I might add). She was carrying two tree trunks full of rocks, a bag of rocks in a bilum bag around her head, and had a baby in a papoose on her chest. And, she easily passed me going uphill. When I got to the foundation to dump my rocks in beside her (she was still there because she had so much more than I did), I emptied my trunk in the pile and watched her finish hers. I then looked at her in awe and admiration and simply said,

"Thank you for helping! You are working so hard!" She looked me square in the eyes and in very broken English but with the biggest most beautiful smile on her face said, "My *pikinini* ("child" in Tok Pisin) will go to school here!"

Jimi's Chief Rock Loader in Papua New Guinea

This simple sentence had the same effects on me as those two words from the Zambian orphans: *Books! Tuition!* I was speechless, amazed, inspired, and more motivated and dedicated to school building than ever. This is it! Hand delivered hope. Hope for their children. Hope for the future. Hope for a better life! That is why the community welcomed us, that is why they were willing to work so hard for this, that is why we built the classrooms in nine days and why the school is continuing to grow and thrive eleven years later. This was the first time I heard this powerful sentence, but now we hear it at least once on pretty much every project. When we thank a parent for working so hard, ask a grandparent why they came out to help, recognize the community for their support, or ask a local official to make a speech, this theme is always a part of it. *Our children will go to school here!* And every time I hear it, I am amazed, inspired and more motivated than ever to keep partnering with local communities to help them build, renovate, and resource schools for their children everywhere that we can.

I had another first in PNG. It was such an amazing experience and I wanted to somehow make it a permanent part of my story and make this community a permanent part of my life as well. I noticed that many of the men and women had tattoos of different types that they apparently did locally and so I asked them about the significance and how they were done. They told me that the tattoos were a very long tradition with different symbolic meanings for different tribes—some signified different stages of life, some identified the family or tribe you were in, some were rewards for hunting or battle prowess, and others were religious symbols. They were all done by hand using "ink" made from ash or char from different burned woods or nuts and made permanent by tattooing the skin using a wood splinter or sharp thorn tapped by hand or with a wood mallet. I asked if someone from outside the community was allowed to get one, and if so, had anyone ever gotten one?

They said it would be okay if a village elder allowed it, but that no one had ever asked to their knowledge. So, I asked who was the best at it and they all pointed to one woman. I asked her if I got permission from an elder, if she would do a tattoo on me. She just giggled. I took that as a tentative *yes* and the next day I asked Martin what he thought and who I should ask. He said the community would actually love it—it would show respect for them and their traditions and that he was sure they would approve. He asked me what tattoo I wanted and I said I would like "BTCV" on my right shoulder. He said, "Yes, let's do that!" Which I thought meant me. But the next afternoon as soon as we were done with work and the rest of the team went to the market, Martin took me to the tattoo lady's house and we both got "BTCV" tattoos done with ash ink and a bamboo splinter needle tapped in by hand. About thirty people watched the process and provided a running commentary of which I understood zero, interspersed frequently with laughing. I am pretty sure a lot of commentary and all of the laughing had to do with how the pitch-black ink looked on my white skin, why I was getting letters put on my back instead of the traditional artwork, if I was tough enough to handle it, and what my wife would say when she saw it.

Well, the last question was answered when she got back from the market—she did not know I was having it done, and when I showed her at dinner, she said, "Wow, that is...um...it is...um...very big." My mom was even less impressed when I showed her months later, but I love it, am very happy I got it, and would definitely do it again (in fact I did do it again four years later when I got "be the change" tattooed under it done by a different PNG tattoo artist but with the same type of ink and needle, all by hand). The tattoos are very unique and they are a symbol of my permanent connection to people I love dearly and who inspire me each and every day.

Martin's hand-done BTCV tattoo to match Jimi's

With a fresh tattoo on my back and more importantly a brand new three-classroom building ready to be christened, it was time for a sing-sing. Like I said, I had heard about these cultural festivals in PNG before we came, but it is something that until you experience it in person, you really have no idea what it is like. Add to this one, that this sing-sing was to celebrate a brand-new school building that seven villages came together to build for their children—their future.

Then, add to all that, the fact that Martin is one of the best and most inspiring leaders and speakers in the known world and you can maybe get a small inkling of what it was like.

More than 2,000 people showed up. The dress, singing, dancing, and music were even beyond *National Geographic's* greatest hits. We were showered with handshakes, hugs, and thank-yous. The village craftsmen hand carved and painted a beautiful sign for the school, naming it *BTCV 003 Brikiti Central Elementary School, Apangai, PNG.* It was, and is to this day, one of the most beautiful things I have seen. The craftsmanship was exquisite and what it symbolized—the collision of two vastly different worlds to birth a place of learning, community, opportunity, and hope—was profound.

The emotions were intense. There was joy, *true joy*, from the community members in celebrating this opportunity for their children and hope for their future and from the team by being part of something so special and meaningful and real and raw. There was awe—for the incredible amount of diversity and depth of talent in PNG people: the traditional dress, singing, dancing, and music were truly extraordinary. All were done without electronics choreographers, perfectly engineered instruments, or roadies. And the artists were from four years old to over seventy years old, and each knew what the dress, song, dance, and music meant, its history, what it signified to the village or tribe, and why they chose it for this sing-sing.

There was appreciation for Changers who were willing to give up vacation time, time with family, the comforts of home, and spend their own hard-earned money to travel sixty-three hours each way to the "land of cannibals, head hunters, and witch doctors" to work incredibly hard to hand deliver hope. I also felt so much gratitude for the thousands of people from seven villages in this remote corner of the world to come out to spend a whole day celebrating the completion of a small building, for making the team feel so valued and appreciated and part of the community, and for caring so deeply about their children's education and future.

There was inspiration from Martin's speech at the sing-sing. Over 2,000 PNGers and a team of Changers were absolutely enraptured, including me. He talked about the importance of education, he said it is not a gift, it is an opportunity that has to be pursued and earned with hard work and passion. He made it clear that this is not "the Americans' school," it is the community's school and they had to appreciate it, maintain it, and sustain it. He implored them to participate in their children's education by getting them to school every day, encouraging them in their studies, and supporting their dreams. He said they had to strongly support the teachers and school administrators. And, he told them that the monthly parent workdays at the school were a must.

Some have said that Martin physically resembles Idi Amin (which I can see), but I can assure you that his heart and his soul fit in the Martin Luther King and Mandela category. Martin just "gets it"—he is a true leader, a dedicated activist, and a Changer. I am so glad we are connected, through BTCV and now a tattoo, and will always be inspired by who he is and what he does. I told him after the speech that I was so inspired that I would run through a brick wall for him. He said, "Oh please no, brother!" Yeah, that one was lost in translation, so I just gave him a big hug and said, "It just means, you're awesome!" He smiled. And, before he could say anything else, we were both whisked away by three village chiefs wearing giant tribal masks who threw us into the giant tribal dance party. We danced, smiled, laughed, ate, sang, and played hand-carved drums until it was dark and everyone had to start walking back to their villages. What an experience, and what an education *I* was getting!

It was extremely hard to leave PNG. It was my first build as a team leader, it was an incredible adventure with an incredible community, it was hard work, it was far away, but oh so very worth it! I left more determined than ever to do more—more projects, more volunteers, more outreach, more awareness, and more fundraising. I was more determined than ever to accomplish my Big Hairy Audacious Goal of completing at least one hundred education-focused development aid projects before I died—it was so clear that the weapon of education is extremely powerful and that we had to use it as much as we possibly could to continue to help people realize their dreams, we had to do more hand delivering hope.

A picture from that build that captures all of that for me and will forever be in my mind is one of Glenn (yep, the same Glenn who worked on the window in Rwanda with Irene, and who later became known to all Changers as "OG"—keep reading). Glenn turned eighty years young on this project and gave his time, talents, and treasures to travel from Columbus, Ohio, to the other side of the world with this fledgling organization to help a small isolated community in PNG build classrooms, *on his birthday*.

The picture is of him standing in front of the newly-completed classrooms, holding the hands of two young Brikiti Central Elementary School students in their blue and white school uniforms. All three of these "youngsters" have their heads held high, their chests puffed out, and ear-to-ear smiles on their faces. In the two weeks they spent together, working hard every day to build a school with each other, they became the best of friends. An "old white American retiree" and two very young black PNG kids who were just getting started in life. While they looked very different in many ways, they actually were very much the same in the most important ways. All three are people on this small planet who care about others, love to learn, and want to create the best possible future for themselves, their families, their communities, and their world. I hope you can see this picture in your mind and I hope it inspires you like it does me.

Several years later, we returned to PNG for the fourth time to complete Omo Community School, our eighteenth project, and Sumuna Elementary School, our nineteenth project. The Sumuna School is located on the tiny, remote island of Djaul. It took a two-hour boat ride, in small skiffs on the open sea, to reach the village. The last part of the journey was down very narrow mangrove-bordered waterways that we had to paddle and push through, looking every bit like the dangerous jungle scene of every action-adventure movie, until we reached the small village where the school was located. As soon as we could see the narrow jungle water path converging to an end, we also saw our welcoming party—more than fifty kids in their bright orange and green school uniforms looking excited, apprehensive, curious, nervous, interested, and scared all rolled into one.

The only white people they had ever seen before were the one or two scouts from various companies who made the trip out there to see what they might be able to exploit from the land or the people in this hidden gem of a forgotten community. So, when we showed up to officially open their new classrooms with them, they were not sure whether to greet us as family they had never known or keep a close eye on us to make sure this wasn't some disguised scheme to get "what we really wanted" from them.

Well, their question was answered and their fears relieved very quickly by Glenn. *Yep, same Glenn.* What I haven't told you yet was that this was the Willett Family Project. Glenn decided that his family wanted to fund this project without ever stepping foot on this tiny island, meeting the community, or talking with the students, parents, or teachers. Don't get me wrong, he did his homework on this project. Glenn is a savvy businessman, an individual of the highest integrity and accountability, and a Changer. He went through every line of the budget, reviewed the construction plans and timelines, ensured the community buy-in was there, and checked the sustainability plan regarding teachers and curriculum. Once he was comfortable with all of this, then he was all in, and the Willett Family Classrooms in Sumuna PNG quickly became a reality.

And what a beautiful reality it was. One of my most treasured memories is of Glenn being mobbed by a very large group of smiling, jumping, giggling, laughing, singing, and truly joyful PNG kids from four to sixteen years of age, all trying to be the one to lead him by the hand on a tour of the Willett Family Classrooms. All I could do was follow from about ten feet back with tears running down my cheeks and my soul smiling, walking on air because of this scene. At least for this moment in time, all was right in the world. *This, is being the change, my friends!* And, *that* is the embodiment of our mission—a white-haired educated, successful octogenarian traveling to the ends of the earth to experience the pure joy of being led by the hand by excited PNG kids with no shoes on their feet, one set of clothes, no running water, and living in hand-to-mouth survival mode, who are more excited than kids on Christmas morning taking him on a tour to show them *their* school that his family had changed for the better.

Fittingly, we got to see a graduation ceremony for the primary school kids and I mentioned to Martin and the other leaders in attendance that I felt like we were celebrating our own kids' hopes and dreams come true. Martin smiled a knowing and contented smile, and simply said, "That is because you are. You belong here!" This may not seem like a particularly earth-shattering response, but it was—at least to me. BTCV always tries to partner with communities, respect the culture, and empathize with our hosts, and I think we have learned to do that well over the years, by learning from the mistakes, the failures, and the successes that you will read more about as you continue. However, one real test of doing this "right" is to no longer feel like outsiders and tourists, but to truly become part of the community—to become family. In that simple phrase, Martin was saying, *you are family*, and we truly felt it and it meant the world to us!

In his graduation speech, when the school principal said he was so grateful that "Americans, from the most powerful country in the world" came to help them, it really hit me hard. We are viewed that way, and it is probably accurate by most measures, but I couldn't help but think that if we are really that powerful, *why aren't we doing more with it—more good with it? Why aren't we building more schools? Why aren't we training more developing-world doctors and nurses? Why aren't we empowering more women in village co-ops? Are we afraid of losing that power? Do we think that power is only maintained through a close-fisted stranglehold rather than an open hand of hope? Are we frightened that other people realizing their dreams will put an end to ours? Are we really that selfish, that foolish, that lost?*

All of these thoughts were bubbling in my mind like boiling water in a tea kettle as I was called up to the "stage" in that little classroom in that tiny village on that small island in that remote part of the globe with a hundred little bright young eyes focused intently on me wondering what the tall "powerful" American who helped bring them new classrooms was going to tell them—when the boiling tea kettle of thoughts exploded into a steam-powered whistle, this is what came out of my mouth:

You said that we are the most powerful nation on earth, which is probably true, but I believe we are only truly powerful if we use that power to help others. If we do not use that power to create opportunity for bright, beautiful, and deserving people like you, we are not only wasting our power, we are becoming weak. The most powerful tool, the greatest opportunity we can share with you is education. Education can make your dreams come true. Education can give you power—most importantly, the power to help others. Please take this opportunity to pursue your education with passion—learn, grow, achieve—become powerful and then use that power for good—to help your family, your community, and your country ... and the world. Be the change you wish to see in the world—through the power of education.

I hope that I will take my own advice. I hope that you will too. After all, *isn't that what family is all about?*

SOUTH AFRICA

So, I am asking you to do something great. Do you have a cause, a passion, a mission that grips your heart and can move you to tears in thirty seconds? If not, you are not fully alive! If there isn't something in your life that is bigger than you, outside of you, not about you, that demands and deserves your time, talent, and treasure, I beg you, don't live like that. We don't have time to simply coast.

— WESS STAFFORD, *Just a Minute*

After we had completed a few school building projects and word got out, I started to get asked to give talks to various groups. As I read through my emails one day, I saw another invitation.

Dr. Cook, you do not know me, but I work with your resident's husband and also know your grant writer's wife. They have both told me about your wonderful work building schools. I teach at Columbia Independent School and one of our classes is called Global Issues. We have guest speakers come in to talk to our students about topics such as free trade, child soldiers, sex trafficking, and resource conservation. Would you be willing and able to talk to the class about your school building work?

Jennifer Anderson

Wait a minute, *you are teaching this to high school students in Columbia, Missouri? And, you want me to be one of the speakers? Why didn't they have this class in my high school?* I definitely would have listened *and* even done my homework for that class! I had never even heard of this school and was not sure this could really be true. So, I asked my resident and my grant writer and they assured me that it was legit. So, I replied:

Sure, I would love to—thank you for the opportunity!

Well, I had no idea what an opportunity it was going to turn out to be. We set the day and time, I gave the talk to nine very interested and engaged high school students, who were incredibly smart and savvy, asked me questions with a depth of understanding well beyond their years, and made me think a lot about how to "do BTCV" better. One of the last questions was from Katy, a sophomore, who was very well-spoken and poised and said, "So, can I go with you?" In my typical respond-without-totally-thinking-it-through manner, I said, "Sure!" Her poise and maturity combined with a fire in her eyes I saw after my answer, made me think, *Dude, she is going to take you up on this and you have never had high school students on a project, have no idea what her parents will say, have no idea what the school will say, and have no idea if it is even really possible.* Oh well, we will figure it out if and when it really happens. (yeah, it's happening).

Fast forward, four months later and I get another email from Ms. Anderson:

Dr. Cook, the culmination of the Global Issues class was to allow the students to "do something" after learning about all the issues in our world and what different people, like you, are doing to address them. They got to choose what to do and who for. They unanimously chose to do a fundraiser and awareness raiser for BTCV. If you are willing, they will work with you and your organization to set this up and see it to fruition. Are you willing to help the students with this? Thank you for considering it!

Are you kidding? "Yes, I am willing, they are helping me, and thank you!"

Fast forward another month and we were at the first *Chili for Change Fundraiser* at Columbia Independent School. It was a chili cook-off fundraiser with live music, educational materials, and a presentation when I got to tell the BTCV story to an audience of students, teachers, administrators, parents, and community members. My talk was well received—and best of all, two more students and two parents asked if CIS students could go with us on a build. Well, you know what my answer was each time: "Sure!" And they did take me up on it—students, parents, and the school. With our blessing, they decided to make it a formal process and offer the opportunity to the rising juniors and seniors through an application process followed by a preparation and fundraising program supported by the school.

Fast forward another ten months and Katy, Abby, Amanda, and Seth, and one of their teachers Mr. Luther, were absolutely beaming as they met Cristi and me at the St. Louis airport on a Friday morning to go to South Africa to help build a school in Mt. Fletcher. Over those ten months, these four incredible students, led by two amazing teachers (Ms. Anderson and Mr. Wally Luther), had completed applications, essays, and interviews with Cristi and me. They and their parents, classmates, and school administrators read books and watched documentaries and movies about South Africa, held multiple fundraisers, raised money on their own by babysitting, mowing lawns, and cleaning, and prepared themselves in every way possible to be Changers. It was incredible for us to see how deeply they took the true purpose of the trip to heart—they definitely did not see this as a "spring break trip" or a posh study abroad experience—they understood that this was an intensive immersion experience in development aid, and they were ready. The other piece of good news was that all their parents were standing there with them with their faces beaming as well. Incredibly, they were also ready and willing to allow their precious children to follow this crazy veterinarian school-builder to a very remote part of Africa—no pressure, right?!

Things started off great—the hugs and goodbyes were nice, I promised to take care of their kids, and our flight left right on time. The layover in Washington DC gave us plenty of time to get some food, meet my sister Janet there, talk about the project, and get to know each other better by playing games, telling stories, and looking at each other's pictures. The flight to Johannesburg came up on the board, we found our gate, and we started getting really excited. And then ...

They called us up to check our passports. The kids got theirs done, Janet got hers done, Wally—yep—no problem. Cristi took ours up and was up there a long time, but I was not really paying attention at first. I did finally notice her being gone awhile and then noticed her waving at me to come up to the counter. I did and walked up to a nightmare. The agent told me that I could not go on the flight because I did not have an empty page in my passport for the visa.

I said, "What, there is plenty of empty space there."

She said, "No, you have to have an entire empty page with no other stamps or stickers on it, you cannot go to South Africa until you do."

I showed her two empty pages in the very back. She said those were not official visa pages. I showed her an official visa page with one very small stamp in the corner with plenty of room for the South Africa sticker. She said that does not qualify. I found a page where a visa was stapled on and removed it and took it back to her, she said that now completely voided my passport and she would not allow me to go. I asked to speak to a supervisor and she refused to let me.

I promise that I will take great care of your kids, I had just told their parents. *How was I going to do that since I would not be going with them?!* This cannot be happening!

I still had an hour and a half until boarding and it was 3:30 EST. *What could I do?* Well, I was in DC, so I figured I would call government agencies.

I called the passport office: recording.

I called the embassy: recording.

I called the South African embassy in DC: recording.

I called the airline: recording.

I called a different passport office number: finally, I got someone!

I explained the entire situation and she said, "You will have to get more passport pages put in your passport at a passport center."

She then let me know there was a passport center right in DC and their first available appointment was ... two weeks from next Thursday.

What? "Is there any other way?"

She said, "You can check for earlier appointments at other passport centers; New York or Chicago would be closest."

SOUTH AFRICA

"You don't understand, I *have* to be on this flight with these kids—I promised their parents!"

"I am sorry sir, there is nothing I can do."

Now what? Do we cancel the trip, all wait until I can go, have the team go without me? I talked with Cristi and Wally and we decided that they would all still go and I would try to figure out some way to get there as soon as possible to join them. I had no idea what that could be, but we called the school principal to let him know, called our contacts in South Africa, and told the kids. To be honest, everyone was a little freaked out, including me, but we all put on our best it'll-be-all-right faces and I started making some more calls to our travel agents, Chicago and New York passport centers, DC hotel (I needed somewhere to stay that night), express passport service in Hawaii (it was still early Friday there), and my Momma (everyone needs their Momma at a time like this, and mine is a true prayer warrior).

I saw the team off—feeling heartbroken, angry, worried, embarrassed and guilty—and took a cab to my cheap hotel and started looking online for every possible avenue of getting one stinking blank page in my passport.

After about forty phone calls, literally hundreds of websites, and probably about fifty emails, my best two bets were either flying to Chicago for an appointment at their passport center on Tuesday and getting to South Africa on Thursday or getting a new passport through the express service in Hawaii to arrive at the DC hotel Monday morning and getting to South Africa on Wednesday. Not only were these both very expensive options, they would wreak havoc with the team's logistics because they would have left Cape Town and been one flight and a six-hour drive away in Mount Fletcher by then. No way was I giving up or giving in though.

Two of my calls were to airlines. South African Airways, the airlines we had tickets with, told me that my flights were still good once I had a valid passport. American Airlines, who I am a platinum member with, had a flight to Cape Town the next day at 1:00 p.m. and I actually had enough miles to pay for that flight. So, these were the best options in terms of cost and logistics as I could still catch the team in Cape Town only a day late, but I needed the passport for South African Airways and I would have to risk American Airlines not accepting my passport for the same reason. After an exhausting and exhaustive effort, I was ready to call it quits for the night and get some rest—I decided I was going to try the American Airlines route in the morning.

Then I remembered something. We had just that week had dinner with our friends Drew and Shari and they were telling us about their longtime friend, Scott Murphy, who had just become a US Representative in New York. I had no idea why I thought he could or would help me, but I decided to call Drew and Shari and see. Shari is an amazing woman who just *gets stuff done*, or GSD as we like to say. As she always does, she immediately sprang into action. She said she would call him right away and let me know. It was after 11:00 p.m. so honestly, I was not expecting her to even get hold of him that night and certainly not get any answers. I went to bed completely exhausted.

Do you believe in miracles? I do.

The next morning, I woke up early, got ready, re-packed, checked email (nothing of significance) and decided I would just head to the airport and hang out there waiting on the American Airlines flight. I figured if I got checked in early it might help get me through and keep all my options open in case that did not work. I just got some coffee and sat down in front of the check-in desk when my phone rang. I answered.

"Hi Jimi, this is Scott Murphy, I am a friend of Drew and Shari Hamilton and Shari told me about your predicament. What's the story?"

I first said, "Wow, thank you so much for trying to help me," and then I told him the very condensed version and what my plans and options were at this point.

He said, "Well, our problem is that it is Saturday, so I don't think I can get anyone to go down to the passport center to open it up and take care of this today, and I am not sure the embassy can do anything to help with this either, but let me make some calls and get back to you." I thanked him again immensely and told him that I would just continue with the current plan.

Typical Shari GSD – she got a US Congressman to call me on a Saturday morning to try to open up a federal agency for me! Really cool – too bad it was Saturday and he couldn't help.

I went back to my coffee and the web, checking sports scores, news, and emails. Even though the situation was bad, I felt really blessed and definitely not alone even though I was by myself at the airport. Maybe thirty minutes later the phone rang again—same number.

"Hi Jimi, this is Scott Murphy again, I have some good news. My aide just informed me that today is National Passport Day. It is the one day of the year where the passport centers are open on a Saturday to encourage people to get their passports. So, we have it all set up for you—you just need to head over to the passport center in the Farragut area—they will be expecting you—just tell them who you are and they will take you in right away and get you some new pages. Do you want me to send my aide over to pick you up and take you there and back?"

"Jimi, are you there?"

"Wha—yes sir, I am here. I am so sorry, I am just in shock, this is a miracle! How ... where is it again?"

"It's on Pennsylvania Avenue—do you want me to send my aide to get you and take you there?"

"No sir, I will take a cab. I cannot thank you enough—this is truly a miracle. I cannot believe you would do this for me. I cannot even tell you how much this means to me, how much this helps, what a lifesaver you are ..."

... continue my rambling in your own mind ...

Then I finally stopped, thanked him again, and asked how I could ever repay this incredible favor.

He said, "I believe in what you are doing! That is more than enough."

I didn't really have time to break down in tears of joy right there and then, so I thanked him one more time and said goodbye.

I went straight out and grabbed a cab to take me to the passport center. As we pulled up to the passport center, I saw the next hurdle in this adventure: a line of people that literally went around the block and down the street. I got out, paid the cabbie, and checked it out. Yes, definitely the line for the passport center. I guess I should not have been surprised, it was the only Saturday of the year that this was open.

I headed toward the back of the line as I am very against cutting in line, but then I remembered Congressman Murphy's words, "*They will be expecting you—just tell them who you are and they will take you in right away...*" So I sheepishly headed toward the front door, trying to stay unassuming and just check it out. When I got near the front door, I saw a uniformed passport agent standing out front looking around. I still could not bring myself to just barge up there and ask if she was waiting for me, so I just pulled the old "inquisitive eye contact routine" to see if maybe she was.

As soon as we "gave each other the look" she said, "Are you Dr. Cook?"

"Yes," I answered, still in a state of disbelief.

She immediately said, "Come with me" and took me in through the exit door, past the front counter, and back to her desk area. She said, "Let me see your passport please." I handed it over, and she said "please wait here" as she walked further into the center. I looked around not knowing what to do. No one seemed to really notice me there as they were all very busy helping other people or working on their computers, so I sat down and waited.

I am not sure how long it was, but it seemed like only two or three minutes when my second angel of the day came back smiling with my passport in her hand. She handed it to me and said "You are all set." It was much thicker than before, but was definitely still my same passport. Elated beyond belief, I said "thank you!" and looked inside—fifty brand new completely blank pages had been inserted. Wow, I really was all set!

I stammered out the most sincere and heartfelt *thank-yous* I could to which she replied, "You are very welcome, I am glad we could help."

A cab ride later, I was back at the airport waiting for South African Airways to open the check-in for my flight. Same flight, twenty-four hours later. I was completely "legal" now, but I still had a great deal of apprehension about whether this was going to work. If I did not get on the flight that night, it would complicate the logistics tremendously as the team would be leaving Cape Town and heading out into the remote area of the Eastern Cape where we would be working on the school. But, surely, the biggest hurdles were overcome and the rest would be smooth sailing, *right?*

Checking my email I saw that the team made it to Cape Town just fine, hundreds of people were praying for me, and Shari was following up to make sure it all worked out. I gave them all the scoop and got geared up for the next steps.

I checked in at the front desk and got the next piece of bad news. The flight was completely full—they could only offer me standby. At that moment, I really did not have the energy or the will to argue, so I just said, "Okay, I'll take it and pray for the best," checked my bag and went through security. Same flight and same gate—I was over two hours early, had no appetite, and didn't really want to leave the gate, so I sat down right by the counter and waited.

When the gate agents showed up about an hour later, I got the next piece of bad news—same agent as the day before. I decided there was no sense in worrying about it or overthinking it so I just waited until they opened for passport check-in and got in line. As she saw me approach her, I could tell she definitely remembered me and in her mind, knew there was no way I could have gotten my passport in order. She was going to uncover whatever scheme I was going to try to pull, kick me off of her flight again, and probably send me to jail for passport fraud. She didn't know about my secret weapon and the miracle that had been performed for me.

I gave her my boarding card (no seat assignment) and passport and she gleefully took it from me to quickly look through it so she could bust me. But, what to her wondering eyes should appear but fifty, *count them fifty*, official blank pages! She looked up in apparent horror and disbelief.

"Wha—?" is all she said.

"National Passport Day," is all I said.

She handed me back my boarding pass and passport and said, "Uh, okay then."

I said, "Thank you so much" and then asked if there was any chance I could get a seat assignment. Now, she had me again! The color rushed back to her face. "No," she said, "the flight is completely full. You will have to wait until it is completely boarded to see if a seat opens up, but I doubt it will." I just said "Okay, thank you, I will wait."

And wait I did—for another hour and a half while over a hundred people boarded the plane that I really needed to be on. I was sitting right by the counter still, praying like crazy, and trying to figure out what I would do next if I did not get on. Every single person in the waiting area was gone—I was all alone—physically and figuratively. The agents at the door were looking around. No announcements, no passengers frantically running to the gate, no final calls. And then…

"Passenger Cook, please approach the desk." I catapulted from my seat like I was shot out of a cannon and ran the fifteen feet to the desk. The same agent was there with a disgusted look on her face holding a boarding pass with a seat assignment… and my name on it! She did not say a word, and that was fine with me—I grabbed it, said "Thank you" (otherwise my Momma would kill me) and said a silent *thank you Lord*! And I floated down the jet bridge to board the flight! I was never so happy to have a middle seat on a twelve-hour flight in my life!

As Al Michaels said after the 1980 US Olympic Hockey Team beat the Russians, "Do you believe in miracles? Yes!"

This covers almost all of this part of the story, but not quite—there was one more hurdle and one more angel. When I got to Johannesburg, I made it through customs and immigration fine (You know where they put the visa sticker, right? On a non-blank page!) then headed over to the domestic terminal to check in and transfer my bags. The line at South African Airways (SAA) domestic check-in was very long and I honestly could not figure out which counter I should go to as there were at least twenty to choose from. I must have looked like I needed some serious help, because a SAA agent who was just walking through looked at me and said, "Do you need help sir?"

I said, "I really, really do please," and gave her the condensed version of my story. She said, "Come with me." She took me to the office area where she worked and got on her computer to get things figured out for me. She typed away for a bit and then furrowed her brow, frowned and said, "Ooh..." That did not sound good to me. It wasn't. She looked up at me and said, "They did not rebook your domestic flights when they changed the international flight." *NO!* I was about to lose it and this third angel could sense that for sure. "My friend," she said, "we will fix it." Somehow, by her empathy and compassion and the grace of God, she *hand wrote* me a ticket on the Cape Town flight, walked me to the security area herself and bid me good luck and safe travels. Well, I could not let it go at that, I had to give her a giant hug and tell her that she had worked a miracle for me and that it would help many kids in her country to have a better education.

She simply said, "I believe you!" And walked away.

I'll ask it again, do you believe in miracles? I do!

I made it! In fact, I made it in time to join the relieved team in Cape Town for dessert at a send-off barbeque that Dominique's sister held for us, and even got to go to World Heritage Site Robben Island with the students the next day to tour the prison where Nelson Mandela was held during the apartheid period, before we headed out to Mount Fletcher.

The Mount Fletcher trip was another "adventure" however. The flight from Cape Town to Durban was no problem. We went to get the rental van and were informed that they did not have the twenty-passenger bus we thought we were getting and instead would have to take two regular vans with trailers. After a bit of polite arguing from Dominique, we learned it really was the only option and we would have to "go with the flow" and make it work. So, we loaded up all the luggage and started piling into the vans.

And then Brian handed me the keys to one of the vans. "Oh, I'm driving one?"

"Yep, just follow us."

I guess I am going to drive a van, with a manual transmission on the left, pulling a trailer, on the "wrong side" of the road, filled with high school students whose parents I promised I would take good care of, in South Africa, for a five-hour trip into the remote area of the Eastern Cape. That is part of *being the change*! Here we go.

Getting into and out of the city was mildly terrifying. My mind was reeling. *Were the pedals on the opposite side too? Were the gears set up backwards? Which way do I look at the stop sign? Which lane do I get in after I turn?* Soon we got out on the open road and I started to get the hang of it and relax a bit. I even let my passengers start talking—quietly.

Then, about two hours into the trip, we went through a series of hills and valleys, and on the uphill sections, they usually had a third lane that was a passing lane for the cars going uphill to get around the slower trucks. We were usually in the slow lane, but on a couple of the longer hills, we went in the passing lane to get around some large semis. As we were approaching the tenth or eleventh hill, we were stuck behind a very slow semi, so when we got to the base of the hill, Brian who was driving the lead van, pulled into the right lane to go around the semi. Unfortunately, this hill did not have a passing lane and Brian had pulled right into oncoming traffic. When he realized it, his instinct was to swerve to his right as you would do in America. The driver of the oncoming truck (UPS-size truck) was South African and his instinct was to swerve to his left, so the avoidance tactics backfired and they hit pretty much head on. I had stayed in the lane behind the truck and so we passed Brian's van right before impact and I will never forget looking over and seeing Dominique's face looking at me from the passenger's seat in sheer panic. It was a horrible thing to see and still gives me chills when I remember it to this day.

We halfway saw and definitely heard the collision and as quickly as I could, I pulled our van to the side of the road and jumped out and started running down the hill. When I got down there, everyone was still in the van and I thought I would need to start carefully getting the injured out of the van and triaging the wounded. I did not have a global plan on my cell phone and I was not sure what number I would call for help. As I got to Dominique's window, the driver of the truck was getting out of his vehicle and walking towards Brian's side of the van. Dominique rolled her window down as I came up.

"Are you okay? Is everyone okay?"

"Yes... yes... I am okay... is everyone okay?"

"Yes we are all okay."

The driver was standing by Brian's door—he had not rolled his window down yet. The rest of the team from my van was arriving now too and hearing and seeing that everyone was okay. I think the strange sight of all these Americans (and one Irishman) of all ages in and outside the van, the relief of no injuries, and Brian then jumping out of the van and immediately profusely apologizing to him made the truck driver more confused than angry. With grave disaster averted, we all started hugging our teammates, assessing the damage, and even mustered a bit of laughter about what a crazy trip this had already been.

Both the truck and the van were drivable, so Brian and the truck driver quickly decided that it would be best to drive to the nearest town to report the accident to police so that the requirements for reporting and insurance were met—evidently, that is how it works in South Africa.

It was about thirty minutes—in the right direction for us, wrong direction for the truck driver—to the nearest town. We pulled up in front of the police station and a crowd quickly gathered. Brian went into the police station with the truck driver while the rest of us gathered by the vans and truck on the street and tried to make sense of everything.

While everyone was a little emotionally banged-up—remember they were fresh off long flights, in a completely different time zone, in a completely different country and culture, away from family and friends, and were just in or witnessed a head-on collision—physically everyone was completely fine. Brian and the truck driver were in the police station a long time. We didn't dare go in and check though as that just did not seem like a smart thing to do. We figured he had to be safe at least, and if he was getting arrested, surely someone would come out to tell us... *wouldn't they?* We decided we could do some things to be efficient while he was in there so we filled the vans up with gas, got everyone some dinner, and continued getting to know each other.

Finally, Brian emerged from the police station with a bewildered look on his face, but quickly conjured up a confident smile and told us, "It's taken care of—let's get to where we are going—I think we missed dinner."

Our destination, Falls Lodge, is off the beaten path to say the least and it took us quite a while to find it in the dark. When we got there, we were not sure it was the right place, but the owner, Adriaan, was outside waiting for us. The lodge was this cool stone-and-plaster South African farm building that conjured up images of Hobbiton from *The Hobbit* with wood-fire smoke puffing gently and peacefully from the chimney. The smoke had the unmistakable smell of home-cooked food. Adriaan had prepared an unbelievable meal for us, that was now about five hours old. But, it still smelled so good and the setting was so unique and inviting that we all abandoned the vans and our baggage and headed straight to the dining area, huddling around the small wooden coffee table there to relive the events of the day and eat an incredible South African stew with the best bread I had ever tasted.

After all of the twists and turns to even get to the actual work of the project, we were especially anxious to just get to work on the school. Finally, day one on the job came with lots of work to do. As usual, we got a tour and then got a game plan together and divided into teams to work on the different parts of the project—I was on the latrine team. Wally, Brian V, Seth and I got our pick-axes and shovels and starting working on digging the trench for the pipe from the school to the latrine pit. It was hot. It was hard work. So, we started singing songs like "I've Been Working on the Railroad," "Hi-Ho, Hi-Ho," and "The Crawdad Song." We had a good rhythm going—singing and digging—and we were kind of in the head-down, get-'er-done mode, when I heard a deep African-accented voice say, "What are you doing?" I looked up to see two South African teenage boys standing there watching us. The one in the green "Gilligan" hat had asked the question. The sun was right above his head as I looked up so it was almost like he was a mirage and I had to blink a couple times to focus in on him and to understand if he really wanted to know what we were doing, if he was messing with us, or if it was just a greeting.

I replied, "We are digging a trench for a latrine."

"Why?" he said

I said, "We are helping to rebuild the primary school here—do you want to help?"

No reply, just a single head-up nod and more watching. We went back to working... and singing.

In between songs, he spoke again, "I like your calves."

"What?"

"I like your calves. How do you get your calves to look like that?"

Now I knew he had to be messing with me—no one ever had told me they like my calves—I have pretty skinny legs, some would even say scrawny.

"Uh, I guess playing basketball and doing work like this—you want to help?"

"Okay, how?"

"You can use the shovel or pick-axe and help like this."

He did and his friend did too. We all tag-teamed it after that and definitely made quicker progress. The conversation went it spurts from there.

"What is your name?"

"Phomotso"

"What is it?

"Phomotso, P-h-o-m-o-t-s-o"

"Famoto?"

"No, P, Pa—Pa-mote-so"

"Got it, Phomotso"

"Right!"

"Do you live around here?"

"Yes."

"Do you go to school?"

"Yes, I go to the secondary school right next to here."

"Where do you live?"

"Right over there." (Points to an actual mud hut just past the edge of campus)

"By yourself?"

"No, with my grandmother."

"What grade are you in school?"

"Grade ten."

"Nice, do you like school?"

"Very much!"

"Awesome! Thanks for your help, you are doing a great job!" A pause while we rotated jobs. "What do you want to be or do for a job?"

"I want to be a photojournalist?"

"Oh cool… wait, what?"

I stopped pick-axing and looked at him. I must have misheard him. This is a very remote part of South Africa. He lives in a mud hut. There are no TVs here, heck, there's not even electricity to the school. The only cameras I have seen are ours. *How can he even know what a photojournalist is, much less want to be one?*

"Sorry, what did you say you want to be?"

"I want to be a photojournalist."

I could not conceal my surprise and skepticism.

"Wow, that's awesome, but how do you even know what that is?"

"We get magazines and I read them all. In the front and under the photos it says who the photojournalists are. I love the photos—each one tells a story by itself. I want to do that."

"That is great Phomotso—do you have a camera?"

"No"

"Well, I will have to introduce you to my wife, Cristi. She is a really good photographer and has a nice camera here."

"Yes please."

As I was working, I got that feeling of being stared at and did not hear the shoveling of Phomotso and his friend anymore. I looked up and in fact Phomotso was staring at me expectantly. The combination of African culture where they typically take what you say literally and his uncontrollable excitement to meet a photographer and see a "real camera" meant that he expected the introduction *now*! Once I understood this and could actually feel the excitement bubbling within him like a kid getting to meet his favorite sports hero, I said, "Right, it is a good time for a break anyway, let's go find her."

"Cristi, this is Phomotso, he wants to be a photojournalist. Can you show him your camera and how to use it?"

"Sure!"

I swear I saw Phomotso glow and levitate at the sights and sounds he just heard. Cristi spent the rest of the afternoon with Phomotso—teaching him about the camera, showing him how to adjust things, and letting him take pictures. He either learned a lot looking at all those magazines, was a natural-born photographer, or both because some of the shots he got were amazing! And, he was on cloud nine—definitely a dream come true for this young man.

Well, Phomotso spent the next two weeks working with us before and after his classes and spending every break from work imbibing as much photography training and practice as was humanly possible. He also got to know the CIS students really well and all of us fell in love with this kid. I think that whole combination melted together in my brain to come up with the idea for Phomotso to come live with us in Columbia, Missouri, and go to CIS for a year so that we could help him pursue his dream.

Phomotso was of course thrilled with this idea when I told him and was hoping, and actually thinking, he could just go back with us. While I certainly did not know all the rules and regulations and details, I did know that could not happen. I could see the look of disappointment and fear come over him when I told him at the dedication and celebration ceremony for the three classrooms, latrines, kitchen, and courtyard we completed with the community that he could not just come back with us. I think it was the "I've-heard-these-promises-before" feeling and the thought that once we leave, we will forget about him. *Yeah, you don't know me, kid!*

Cristi showing Phomotso how to use her camera

So, the process was: contact him as soon as home, have a call with his father, find out where and how he could get a passport, get a passport (three trips to Durban), find out where and how he could get a visa, get a visa (three more trips to Durban), meet with CIS administration, get his transcripts, apply to CIS, submit application for scholarship, another call with his father, figure out flights, book flights, get him to Columbia, Missouri.

Remember two things: 1) this kid had never been out of South Africa, and 2) Cristi and I had never been parents and we were going to start with a sixteen-year-old South African. *What could go wrong?*

Phomotso did get all the above done and came to live with us. He went to CIS, met some amazing people who helped him grow and learn, and went back home to pursue his BHAG. He applied to the photojournalism school at one of the most prestigious universities in South Africa and was granted an interview with the admission committee. With his instant-camera-drugstore-printed-construction-paper-portfolio, his eloquence and charm, and his education, he impressed the committee and was accepted into the photojournalism program. It still gives me indescribable joy and pride to type those words.

Phomotso came to visit us every year, spending time with his "American parents," visiting friends, and experiencing more of the US—and always taking pictures that told a story. During one of the breaks in his last year at university, he also went on a BTCV project in Malawi with us. It was so incredible to spend time with him on a school build—seeing him go from a *BTCV Kid* to Changer and pour his heart, soul, and sweat into helping others who were "just like him" was fulfilling and inspiring. He worked hard, played hard, and of course, took some of the most amazing story-telling pictures the world has ever seen. Someone on the team also snapped a picture of Phomotso, Cristi, and me with our BTCV work shirts on, arms wrapped around each other, and huge smiles on all our faces—that is my favorite and most cherished family picture of all time.

And, he completed his degree in photojournalism! His BHAG came true and I was all set to see him graduate. I was booked to fly to South Africa early on a Saturday morning when I received a call on Friday evening from his best friend, Thato, telling me Phomotso had passed away. Three days before his graduation ceremony, an undiagnosed, asymptomatic heart condition caused him to die in his sleep. We were in shock. Devastated. Lost. Broken. And, while we are still brokenhearted, we know that he accomplished his dream and changed so many lives along the way. Our South African son was a true Changer who left a legacy of passion, positivity, and love that will never be forgotten. Because of him, we learned how to be parents, we learned that true family has little to do with genetics and nearly everything to do with sharing life together, and we learned that miracles really do happen and that a simple conversation, a willing heart, and one person who cares and asks "How can I help?" can start a ripple effect that can change the world.

I need to write my next book all about Phomotso because he was an amazing young man who changed our lives and changed the world for the better in so many ways in his short time on this earth.

In the meantime, I hope that you will take the time to read his story and see some of his work on our website bethechangevolunteers.org. He taught us so much about life, love, hope and dreaming big dreams.

NEPAL

He is no fool who gives what he cannot keep to gain what he cannot lose.

—Jim Elliot

Wow, this is all going so well—this school building stuff is pretty easy. This is definitely what I was thinking at this point and you know what they say about pride going before a fall. Well, *look out below!*

Word was getting around the community, the country, and even the world about BTCV. And, this global word-of-mouth "advertising" led us to an American woman who was working with an orphanage and a number of street kids in Katmandu, Nepal. She contacted us about helping these kids by building a school in the small village in the foothills of the Himalayas that they were displaced from, which sounded like a perfect next project. So, when she told us the story, showed us pictures, and asked for our help, we were convinced and said *yes* right away. This chapter is mostly a full-transparency-please-learn-from-our-mistakes confessional, so I am going to list the major mistakes we made right from the start so you will make sure to take those away as you read the details in the story:

The only contact to the village we had was an American whose heart was in the right place but whose methods were not, and she was not an engaged local community member.

We did not do our own homework on the contact, the community, or the project.

We did not do a site visit and engage the local community.

We said yes right away, immediately did all of the planning, fundraising, and built a team and were on the ground within three months.

There definitely was a lot of good that came from this project and we did learn some of the critical lessons we needed to this way, but

I will let you know that it was painful, scary, hard, and ended up being a project that was not sustained. Hopefully, if you are doing development aid, or similar work, you will learn these lessons from reading about our mistakes and not experiencing them yourselves.

Before we get into the details of the story, I have to say that the brave (and crazy) people that joined this ill-fated team and went on this project were, and are still (believe it or not), a truly amazing group of Changers who we will forever be grateful to and should proudly wear the T-shirt saying *"I survived the BTCV Nepal Build!"*

The project started out well enough—everyone arrived in Katmandu on time with smiles on their faces and strength in their bones. The only minor incident for this portion of the trip was that James' bag came down the baggage claim conveyor belt ripped pretty much in two followed by each article of clothing one piece at a time—including her underwear. But, she took it completely in stride and we all laughed about it!

The first day and a half was pretty awesome too—we met the kids, toured the city, which is an incredible experience, and took the flight over the Himalayas, which is breathtaking. We had some great meals and did some team bonding, which would prove critical later on this trip. Then, the adventure really began.

It was time to head out to the village. Our contact (we will call her Tina) who had worked with this community for the past four years told us she had everything organized. We would take some supplies out with us in the "bus" and the trip should take about four to five hours. The team was packed (we duct taped James' bag back together—part of the team bonding) and ready to go. We had a very early breakfast and headed out to the street to pack the "bus" that was "on the way" with our bags and tools, the supplies that were coming on another truck, the water for the two-week build, and seventeen team members.

After about forty-five minutes, the supplies truck finally pulled up. It was a small flatbed truck loaded up with drain tubes, cement pans, rebar, spare tires and two small septic tanks. Then, our "bus" pulled up—it was a standard twelve-passenger van!

"Uh, Tina, is this it?"

"Yeah, but I will be coming later with some people from the orphanage so you will have one less person to worry about."

"You are not coming with us? Does the driver know where to go?"

"Yeah, for sure—he is from the village."

So now we only have to fit sixteen people in the twelve-passenger van with all our bags and the supplies—*no problem, right?* This team was amazing. I delivered the news in my best it'll-be-all-right voice and what-an-adventure-this-will-be pep talk, and they got right to work. They strapped everything possible on the roof, put the bags under the seats and in the aisles and we all packed in, sitting on bags, water bottles, and each other and off we went.

Mark, who was in front and never met a stranger, tried to strike up a conversation with the driver. Now, based on the tenor of this trip, I bet you can guess how much English the driver spoke. *Yep, zero!* But Mark still tried. He got him to understand the question of how far it was to the village, we thought, and the driver said "two" and held up two fingers. Mark continued, "Two hours?" The driver replied "Two." Hopefully he meant two hours, which if so, was awesome. We all took it as two hours and were filled with hope and that giddy sense of adventure that you get on a school field trip or church choir trip. *This will be fun! No worries!*

Then, the worries started. First, the traffic going out of the city was bumper to bumper, horns honking, and people yelling like the combination of a Brazilian football game and the New York Stock Exchange at the opening bell. Then, the road leaving the city, while featuring truly awe-inspiring scenery, was the most treacherous any of us had ever seen. It was more winding and steeper than the world's craziest roller coasters, with no shoulders on the road and every make, model, and size of vehicle trying to get there yesterday. This made for both physical and mental anxiety, to say the least.

No exaggeration—literally every mile there was a vehicle off the road into the side of the hill or down the mountain that had to have involved a fatality. Let's just say no one called "shotgun" on this trip!

Well, we made it out of the city—intact and alive—still packed in like sardines, a little less giddy and a little more worried. Mark, asked his new best friend, the driver, "how far now?"

"Two."

Great. Now we were wondering if that meant two days, two vehicles, or two drivers. Or maybe it was too far, too many questions, or too risky to tell. Or maybe that was just the only English word he knew. Whatever the case, we tried to settle in, get to know each other better, talk about the scenic flight, the city, or anything else we could think of to pass the time and take our minds off things.

The trip was going pretty well for about four hours—we knew "two" did not mean two hours by this point and the driver made a stop for gas, bathrooms, and snacks. It was nice to stretch and get some Nepalese junk food and feel like we were making progress. *Surely, it could not be too much farther?* When we got back in the van, Mark asked again. *You guessed it.*

"Two."

Well, about two hours later, the asphalt road turned into a semi-asphalt road and then into a dirt road and then nothing. Seriously, the road just stopped. The driver looked very perplexed, stopped the van, and looked back at us. The team looked back at me (I was in the back row of the van). After a few minutes of silent bewilderment on everyone's part, I said, "Okay, let me out and I will go try to figure this out." Yes, this was definitely a stall tactic, but what else was I going to do. There was literally nothing around and all that was in front of us was a giant, and I mean giant, pile of dirt and sand and an abandoned bulldozer.

I got out and looked around—the new view produced no differences or solutions. It was afternoon—full sun, hot. One by one, everyone else got out of the van, partly to stretch their legs and partly to see if this was real and if we were now stranded in Nepal's middle-of-nowhere. The driver got out and started walking up the last part of the "road" which turned into the giant dirt-sand pile. I wasn't really sure if he was done with us and heading out on his own or looking for a way forward. The Changers were trying to figure out the surroundings, cracking jokes about last wills and testaments, wondering where Tina was, and wondering how I talked them into this "adventure"—all still with smiles on their faces, believe it or not. John, an Irish contractor on his second project with us, headed toward the bulldozer.

Meanwhile the driver came back and we began a game of how-do-we-get-outta-here charades. It took us awhile, but as a team, we won the jackpot and figured out that he was going to try to drive the van around the giant dirt-sand pile and we were going to push the van so that we could hopefully get around it and back to some semblance of a road. At least we were pretty sure that is what he was signaling to us—either that or he was trying to tell us that he was driving away and to stay at the back of the van or we would get run over—either way, at least we had a plan.

The driver got in, the team positioned ourselves at the back of the van, and we were off. *Hey, it's working!* The van is going up, up, up and around... and then not! Tires spinning, dirt-sand in our faces, exhaust fumes in our lungs, and no road in sight. The good news was we actually made it about one-third of the way up the giant dirt-sand hill and the driver seemed pretty encouraged. In fact, he was starting round two of the charades.

"Oh, oh, I got it," someone yelled. "Take all the stuff off the roof and the luggage out and try again." That got us about another 300 feet, with three tries, but then we were stuck, dirty, and smoked out again.

Now the driver looked very discouraged and the team was starting to feel the same way. It was looking pretty grim as once again the gazes—still friendly thankfully—turned to me. As I was contemplating how I could pull the proverbial rabbit from my hat, John the Irishman, did it for me. As I looked back to where we came from, John was leading the bulldozer—with an operator from who-knows-where following his every directive—up the hill toward us like he was a valet at a Hollywood premiere showing someone where to park. I literally had to rub my eyes to make sure I was not dreaming, but seeing the open-mouthed expressions of my teammates told me it was real. In typical John-fashion, he didn't stop to talk or explain, he just led the dozer around the van and showed the dozer operator where to make a new road for us. That's right—Super Irishman John made us a new road in the middle-of-nowhere Nepal so we could get on with the adventure.

Once we all came to our senses, we repacked the van as quickly as we could, re-sardined ourselves, and followed John and the dozer on our newly-made road for about a quarter of mile until we hooked up with another semi-road and could be on our way. No kidding, John simply gave the dozer operator a nod, jumped in the van, and off we went. I think the combination of pure awe and the desire to keep this story as incredible as it really is prevented us from asking John to explain everything right then and there. Of course we did ask later, and in his humble way with his Irish brogue, John just said, "Aww, I just kindly motioned, I did." Enough said.

We got back on a semi-road, which was not too bad and started driving at a decent pace again. Everyone's spirits were lifted and the joking and storytelling were in full force again. Mark asked the driver, how long now. *You guessed it.*

"Two."

Actually, only a little over an hour later, as the sun was getting low in the sky, we stopped beside what looked like a half-finished house and outbuilding at the top of what appeared to be a steeply descending hill. The driver turned around in his seat for round three of charades. This one was pretty easy—hand pointing down with two fingers doing the walking motion. So, we got the answer quickly and easily but definitely were not sure why we were walking, how far we were walking, and where we were walking to.

With everyone unloaded and circled up at the front of the van, it was time for round four.

"Walk down the hill?" Driver nodding yes.

"Drive, driver, car, bus, *big bus*!" Driver nodding yes.

"Rock a baby, carry a baby, carry something, *carry our bags*!" Driver nodding yes.

"Carry our bags down the hill to a big bus?" Driver nodding yes.

Whether he understood us or not, we proceeded to get our bags, and walk down the hill. *But, wait a minute, what about the supplies?* Our turn for charades. We pointed to all of the stuff on the roof and still stuffed in the van. The driver shook his head no and pointed to the half-finished house and out-building. *Okay, I guess.* We had much bigger things to worry about at that point, like *how far are we going, where is this big bus, is there a big bus, and are we about to meet our Maker?*

We walked down the hill, which was quite a ways, in single file, peering into the early evening half-light with curiosity and apprehension. The apprehension was heightened by the first thing we saw: a river. *Not good.* The only thing I could think to do was to keep walking. Down the hill we went towards the river. No sign of a big bus. No sign of a bridge. No sign of Tina.

Why the team continued to follow me, I will never know, but they did. As we got closer, we did see a bridge...kind of. There was a very rickety log bridge that went halfway across the river. This part of the bridge did have wooden flooring and some form of handrails made from branches strapped together. From the halfway point to almost the other side were just the logs and then the last twenty feet or so were just large rocks. Besides the fact that the bridge looked pretty questionable, we did not see anything or anyone on the other side of the river. There was a path heading up from the landing area, but where it went and what we would find by taking it were still in question. But the alternatives did not seem so great either, so I crossed over to make sure it would not collapse or shift and then went back to the end of the logs to grab bags and arms as the rest of the team crossed over.

Everybody made it without falling in and actually thought it was pretty fun—*what a team!* When we gathered our senses and our bags, we headed up the hill. As we crested the hill of the river bank, it widened into a dirt road and literally as soon as we got to the top we saw headlights facing us. *It was a big bus*! And, there was a driver, and a few other passengers—all Nepalese. The bus driver motioned to us, so naturally we got on. It was a large school bus type vehicle, painted a bunch of different colors, inside and out, with the typical school-bus bench seats. We all went to the back of the bus, holding our bags and backpacks, stuffing what we could in the overhead racks or underneath the seats, and stacking the rest in open seats. We really didn't say much to the driver or each other before the bus took off, turning around in about a twenty-five-point turn, and heading off, billowing diesel smoke like an old-time train engine.

We didn't drive too far before we made a stop. At this stop we picked up eight passengers—all Nepalese—and all toting something other than common baggage. Two had chickens in cages, two had chickens out of cages, one had a big bundle of plant stalks of some type, another had two big burlap bags of something, and two had small babies in their arms. We quickly realized we had to reorganize our packing to get this menagerie loaded up. Our new passengers were patient and helpful and did not seem to mind sitting next to or on top of our bags. The trade-off was that we got to help hold the chickens and the babies. No kidding, they just handed us the chickens and their babies like we were family and we settled in for the next part of the journey.

There was one more stop with similar, although less, onboarding, rearranging, and wordless smiling and nodding to get settled. James and I were both still holding "our" babies and both little ones seemed quite content, with the only negative being the streams of snot running down their faces and onto us.

I am actually not sure how long the bus ride was, but it was definitely pitch dark when we pulled into a village. It was clear that this was the end of the line, so we passed the babies and chickens back to their rightful owners, gathered our things and disembarked to determine where we were and if we had farther to go to get to the village we were supposed to be in.

Well, our faith and perseverance were rewarded—when we got off the bus, there was a group of Nepalese villagers waiting for us. We were pretty easy to pick out as you would imagine and so they came right up to us, helping us with our luggage, and saying,

"Tina friends?"

"Be change?"

"Welcome, *namaste!*" They led us to a small, two-story wood house at the far end of the village and took our things inside. As soon as we opened the front door we saw bed mats completely covering the dirt floor of the main room. There were two cots in the corner and a door at the far end of the room.

Our host said, "You sleep here and there and one more," as he pointed to the main room floor, the other door and then at the ceiling.

There was a back room with more bed mats and an upstairs with some thick blankets. Partly because we were exhausted, but mostly because it was an incredibly willing and dedicated team, we quickly figured out who would sleep where—most of the team in the main room, Gary and John on the cots, young women in the back room, and the two couples upstairs. In relief and exhaustion, we all threw our sleeping bags in the respective sleeping areas and crashed.

I wish I could say that it was an uneventful build from there, but that would be very far from the truth.

Tina did show up—the next day. How she got there and if she had any struggles, I personally never found out. I was too tired and too upset to listen to the story if there was one. She would disappear at least once a day though—again, too tired and upset to find out where or why. And she did very little, if any, work. Besides bringing this project to us, she did make one other major contribution—after a morning of sixteen Changers digging with picks and shovels, it became obvious to us that we could spend the whole two weeks digging by hand and not even get close to getting just the foundation done.

Super Irishman John came to me a bit exasperated to make this problematic situation clear to me in full Gaelic color. I knew if John was feeling defeated, then us mere mortals were in trouble and I had to do something. So, I found Tina and asked her if there was any way we could get some type of heavy machinery there to help, thinking it was an impossible ask on the scale of asking Heat Miser for snow in Southtown.

Believe it or not, she said there was "a machine" in the next village—*we can go ask*. I said, "that would be great, but how would we get there?"

She said, "We can drive. I will get the truck."

What truck? About fifteen minutes later, a pretty new Range Rover showed up with a driver and she and John (I insisted he go with her) were on their way. Even more amazing, about an hour later, the Range Rover showed back up followed by a large backhoe with John in the driver's seat. Needless to say, we got the foundation done!

We still had to absolutely work our butts off every day though—it was a really hard project with lots of digging (even with the backhoe), lots of shoveling and hauling rock and sand up the hill from the riverbed, tons and tons and tons (literally) of mixing, transporting, and pouring of cement. And, in the foothills of Nepal, the building had to be earthquake-safe, which meant very deep footers and a thick foundation with lots of rebar. And, it was all at altitude—6,600 feet above sea level to be exact.

Luckily, there were some truly amazing villagers who were passionate about this project, grateful for our partnership, and could speak enough English that we could figure out what to do, how to do it, and how to survive. There was one young husband and wife team, Krishna and Reshma, who were just incredible. They worked so hard, cared so deeply, and always had smiles on their faces. They each outworked us four to one (at least) all day long and then would go home, fix their dinners, take care of their kids, and take care of their own house and rice paddy. I remember Erin saying to the team after about the third day of seeing them do all this with huge smiles on their faces, "*Now, that is a true power couple! The rest of the world has it all wrong.*"

Krishna and Reshma validated this statement and more through their work and their words. Near the end of the build, I thanked them, told them they inspired me, and said we can never repay you or thank you enough for your work, your friendship, your smiles, and your kindness. Krishna smiled a wide, genuine, missing-tooth grin and said, "But you have—you have built the future for the children!" Reshma smiled a bigger grin and simply said, "*Namaste!*"

We ate our meals in what we affectionately called "The Corral." Right outside the front door of the house we were staying in was a very small "courtyard" that was loosely framed to about a five-foot-height with built-in bench seating—it really did look like a corral for people. And, it took on more of that feel from the very first breakfast we had there because the villagers came at every meal time to "view the strange animals" in the corral. It was a bit unnerving, heart-wrenching, and guilt-inducing at first, but we quickly adapted and had fun with it. We invited the kids to come inside the corral to share our benches and our food and would talk with the adults as much as the language barrier allowed. Like everything else on this project, the team took it in stride and turned a negative into a positive.

The Corral also provided me with some additional duties on this project—once the villagers saw me patching up some of the team's minor cuts, bumps, and bruises, it became the village first aid center and veterinary clinic. We ended up providing first aid for a number of things, distributed antiseptic brushes to help treat ringworm in adults and kids and dogs and cats, fixed a broken leg in a very small kitten, and addressed a young boy's badly injured finger. Cristi was my "nurse" and Doug was my "anesthetist." Except it was actually anesthesia by entertainment—Doug, Glenn's fifty-something-year-old son, has an amazing gift of being able to make any person of any age in any culture laugh uncontrollably—and that is what he would do for all our lunchtime visitors.

Once we figured out the problem through translators, sign language, and charades, and made a plan, Doug would go into action. While Cristi and I provided whatever first aid we could, Doug would go into full theatrical genius. He figured out the chink in everyone's laughter armor and would do whatever it took—he would turn his hat sideways, make the funniest faces, create dance moves worthy of *Napoleon Dynamite* and *Saturday Night Fever* combined, and perform slapstick that the Three Stooges would be proud of—anything to get their mind off the pain, the treatment, and the fear so that they, and we, could get through it and get them some initial help. He even got the kitten to pay attention to him.

Unfortunately, we did not do such a great job with our own ailments. Everyone except the three South Africans on the team got really and I mean *really* sick at some point during the trip. I think it was most likely because we listened to Tina who told us that the tap water from the well was "completely safe" to use for brushing teeth. But, in fairness, it could have also been the rats that shared our cooking water barrel (I had to retrieve two of them that drowned in it after a couple of very alarmed Changers found them in there at night) or the rats crawling on us at night (Manny and I both woke up once during the trip to a Nepalese rat on our chests staring us down eye to eye).

Fortunately, the sickness went through us in a wave rather than all at once, so there were always a few of us who could get out of bed, do the work that needed to be done, and take care of the others. The worst and most scary sickness was at the end of the trip when James got extremely ill the night before we were leaving to come home. She progressed from nausea to violent flu-like symptoms to nearly comatose. It was so severe and serious that we discussed admitting her to a hospital in Katmandu or arranging for an emergency medical evacuation. With her making some slight, transient rallies, we decided to try to at least get her to Hong Kong, then at least to Los Angeles, then at least St. Louis... then home. With some electrolyte fluids, several medications, a lot of help and explanations from Erin (another GSD woman) through airport customs, and the most fervent and passionate prayers I have ever prayed, we made it home alive. But, it took her about three months to fully recover.

After surviving to the first Sunday, we walked to the most intriguing little church you could imagine—set in the foothills of the Himalayas with a breathtaking view of the mountains, the terraced rice paddies, the village huts, and the streams coursing through this incredible "top-of-the-world" landscape. Our co-parishioners were mostly kids and chickens (literally), both of whom were quite active during the service, and we did not understand one word the minister said. But, as we so often experience in these village churches, the authentic pure joy permeated us such that we all felt God in a way that was unique and profound. I don't think any of us realized that we had been there over two hours when the benediction came. I know none of us will forget that experience.

Another unforgettable experience was the last evening of the project. We had a wonderful celebration that was so genuine, special, and fun—we played guitar, sang, ate, exchanged gifts, and danced. The "young folks," including Glenn and Doug of course, continued into the wee hours of the morning. Ordinarily, everyone would be upset with being kept awake by the party animals, but the pure joy and jubilation we could hear—and feel—made us all lie on our mats with smiles on our faces.

All in all, it was a really, really tough build, but we survived, got the job done, made lifelong friendships, and had experiences that only a handful of people in the world ever will, which changed us all for the better. And, of course, we got all of our major mistakes and lessons learned out of the way, *right?* Well, not exactly. We had other major, scary lessons to learn in Kenya as you will find out. But the Nepalese lessons have definitely shaped our organization in important and lasting ways. All of the "survivors" of this project are still involved in BTCV, and although the building is not currently functioning primarily as an educational facility, it is used as a community center for the village that does provide resources for this tiny little village in the foothills of the Himalayas, including for Krishna and Reshma and their children.

For me, the biggest lesson from Nepal was that while we absolutely do want to *be the change we wish to see in the world*, we need to see it with the eyes of the local community we are trying to serve, ensure that we have local leader communication, buy-in, and support, and know what we are leading a team of people into before we just "boldly go" and figure it out along the way. You will see that we didn't learn these lessons in one go—*I sure hope you will though.*

ETHIOPIA

"If we are to teach real peace in this world...we shall have to begin with the children."

—MAHATMA GANDHI

"Where are you headed?" the cab driver asked me in his heavy accent that I could not quite place as I got into his cab in downtown San Diego and asked to go to the airport.

"Cambodia," I replied.

"Well, that is not a location I hear every day—what is in Cambodia for you?"

"A school to help build."

"Oh? For who?"

"For a floating Vietnamese village on Tonle Sap Lake."

"What? Why? With who?"

"The Vietnamese in Cambodia live in floating villages on a large lake and they really need a floating school for their kids. My wife and I helped start an organization called *Be The Change Volunteers* that builds schools for deserving communities in need."

"Wow! Can you help my village in Ethiopia?" (Ah, that is why I did not recognize the accent—not one of the more common ones I hear).

"I hope so. Give me your contact info and we will see what we can do when I get back."

"Oh, yes, here it is. Thank you so much!"

Fast forward a year and a half later, more than 500 emails, the death of one of Brian's dear friends and fellow Habitater, a major fundraising effort, building an international team, and we were headed to Afar, Ethiopia.

This was the first time on a build that I felt that I was on another planet. In all the remote and not-so-remote areas of the world I had visited so far, while there were some striking and wonderful differences, I actually had always been astonished, and comforted, by how not-so-different most things really looked. That all changed on the way to Afar. To me, it was like a combination of moonscape, Dante's inferno, and Road Runner cartoon scenes all rolled into one. It was fascinating, exciting and unnerving. Add to it that we were in Land Rovers that were being driven at a very high rate of speed, the temperature kept rising, and we frequently passed semis pulling open-air trailers containing camels packed in very tightly and looking very unhappy (although I admit that I am not sure what a happy camel looks like), and you can understand the out-of-place feeling we all had.

We arrived in Semera, Afar, Ethiopia to help build a library for a remote primary school in memory of Duraid, a dear friend of Brian's, who was a beautiful soul who passed away far too early. We got to know him when he was a member of the Cambodia build, and like everyone else who spends time with him, we immediately fell in love with his incredibly kind heart, quick wit, profound intellect, and great sense of humor. He had always wanted to do some development aid work in Ethiopia and when my taxi cab driver had a connection to this same school that Brian found through a Habitat connection in Addis Ababa in the country that our departed friend and fellow Changer wanted to build in, we knew it was divinely ordained. The other sure sign it was meant to be is that we were readily able to raise funds and build a great team from friends of Duraid and people who heard his story and the BTCV story.

So, there we were, in 110-plus degree heat, in what felt like a sand storm, on planet Moonscape-Inferno-Road-Runner ready to build a library from the ground up. And we did—we fought the heat, the sand, the lack of water, and the limited resources to build a beautiful library that honors the life and memory of a beautiful man, and provided a much-needed resource to more than 300 Ethiopian children.

True to the surroundings, the build was peculiar as well. We found out by meeting several that Rastafarians actually have their roots in Ethiopia (Bob Marley songs became our work songs as we joined in singing with the lead carpenter). We learned that teeth filing or sharpening is still an honored custom among some of the tribes in Afar. We were awoken each morning to a loud *Adhan*, or Islamic call to prayer, broadcast over huge speakers on a tower. And, we learned that if you did not like *injera* and *wat* (Ethiopian curry and spongy flat bread), then you were pretty much out of luck for eating much on this project.

Unfortunately, I found out quickly—on bite number one—that I do not care for injera and wat. Combine that with the facts that most other Ethiopian dishes contain onions which I am very allergic to, we did very hard physical labor in the extreme heat, and I blew out a disc in my back moving massive rocks for the foundation, and it is no wonder I ended up losing eighteen pounds in a little under two weeks on this project.

The disc issue caused me to have to fly home as soon as the work was done while the rest of the team was headed to the sightseeing portion of the trip. It was a very long, very painful, very frustrating trip home, and Cristi definitely earned sainthood (yet again) for getting me through it. We literally went straight from the airport to the orthopaedic institute where I work, so my colleague and friend, Dr. Ted Choma, could examine me—his immediate reaction of, "You look *horrible!*" told me that neither the weight loss or the pain was a good thing—and so he got me set up for an epidural. After the epidural, we went straight to Taco Bell where I ate enough for four people, at least. The epidural helped, but I ended up having surgery a couple months later, which *really* helped.

Ethiopia was also peculiar with respect to the celebration ceremony. First off, it was held in the darkest, hottest, and smallest building on the campus. We never figured out why they chose that building. Brian and I gave our speeches, both thanking them for their hospitality and partnership—Brian honoring Duraid, the donors and the team—and me encouraging parents and grandparents to foster and support their kids' education, and the students to use the power of education to pursue their dreams with passion. Then, the headmaster and a local government official who we had never met before delivered very long speeches about how superior Ethiopia and Ethiopians were to America and Americans, especially in terms of how much more they had done with very little resources.

While some of it may have been accurate, unless something was lost in translation, it came across as pretty pretentious, arrogant, and demeaning, not to mention somewhat ungrateful and rude. Needless to say, there was quite a bit of uncomfortable shifting—from the speeches and the heat—and avoiding of eye contact all around.

As you can tell, we were still working on learning the lesson of ensuring mutual understanding and shared mission with local leadership during the planning process and before being onsite. I guess some lessons just have to be learned the hard way—again and again.

Thankfully, the second speech finally ended to a half-hearted smattering of applause, and it was time for the kids to perform. The Ethiopian kids made everything right in the world again. It is funny and comforting that no matter where you are in the world—kids are kids—especially when they are performing for adults. You have the ones that are so polished and precise that you feel like they have been performing all their lives and could step onto the world's biggest stage to perform an acapella solo without a single jitter or drop of sweat. Then you have the ones that are oblivious to the audience—they look around, play with their clothes or their neighbor's hair, twirl, sit down, and or pick their noses during the majority of the performance. Then you have the clowns, my personal favorite, who are doing everything possible to take the very serious performance and turn it into a laugh-fest for all involved. I absolutely love it when they even get the teacher, leader, conductor, and or headmaster to laugh—*ah, sweet victory for comedy reigns again!*

After the kids danced, a professional group danced—which was very entertaining—and then they got everyone to dance. It was a wonderful experience of in-the-moment cultural exchange, mutual understanding, and shared mission—even though the philosophical togetherness was later than it should have been and the physical togetherness made it even hotter and more claustrophobic in that room—the smiles began appearing on everyone's faces like popcorn popping in the microwave and all the uncomfortableness from the speeches was quickly swept away by the music and the laughter. It was another good build in the books and I am sure Duraid was smiling, laughing, and dancing with us in spirit.

In full transparency, BTCV has not returned to this school to see for ourselves how, or even if, this library is impacting this very remote school on planet Moonscape-Inferno-Road Runner (which is another lesson learned and remedied for subsequent projects). But we have received a number of emails over the subsequent years from my San Diego cab driver, who always thanks us profusely and tells us what a difference we made in his community for which he will be eternally grateful and indebted to us. I never told him about my blown disc or the speeches, and never had the heart to directly respond to his consistent queries in the emails about whether we liked the food or not. Some things are better left unsaid so we can focus on the truly important things in life.

MALAWI

Hope is a powerful weapon and no one power on earth can deprive you of it.
—Nelson Mandela from a letter to Winnie Mandela.
Written on Robben Island, June 23, 1969

"Jimi, I am so sorry, but I just got a call from work and I am not going to be able to go on the build," Debbie told me in a disheartened phone call just three weeks before leaving for Lilongwe, Malawi for build 009.

Debbie is an on-site disaster claims adjuster for a major insurance company and so spur of the moment job assignments are her life. She told us about this possibility when she signed up, but she said she had never seen or heard of anyone being called from a planned vacation in her forty years with the company, so we were praying that this would not be the first time—because most importantly, it meant there was a major natural disaster in the US, and also that she could not go on the build. *But it did and she couldn't.*

Interestingly, I had recently had lunch with a former student's husband who wanted to ask me a favor. This guy, Grant, had been doing some mission work in India with his father, at a school his family and church had built with local partners. The school community wanted to add a soccer field and playground, and a couple of their donors had offered to fund the project. Over lunch, he told me all he was asking of me was if we could assist him by collecting the donations through BTCV and then wiring the money to the school. He said it would be a BTCV project then and he would give a portion of the funding to BTCV for our efforts in this. I told him that he did not need to give BTCV any of the money—that this project was completely on mission for us and that our promise is that one hundred percent of donations go directly to the purpose that donors intended them for. I only asked one thing in return—that he engage local volunteers to work on the project with him. This all intrigued him, so our "quick lunch to ask a favor" turned into a long lunch to have an enthusiastic and impassioned conversation about school building, faith in action, toxic charity, and fundraising. He asked about my vision for BTCV and if that ever included employees, and I shared that it did hopefully, if and when we could get specific funding for that, and of course ended it by telling him he needed to come on a build! He said he was definitely interested.

I don't believe in coincidence or fate. I do believe in divine intervention and miracles as I have already told you, and I think if you finish this chapter that you will see this was another one of those.

Debbie continued, "I don't want any refunds or credits—just use whatever you can for the project, the team, the community and BTCV please."

You will come to learn that Debbie is one of the most giving, generous, and lovely souls that God ever put on this earth. And, don't worry, at the time of writing this book, Debbie has been on twenty-one builds, become our Executive Coordinator of Change, and is known around the world as Debbie Poppins (keep reading), Debbie Mama, and a Changer of the highest distinction.

I replied, "Debbie, oh no! You're kidding! I am so disappointed for you and us! And, you are so amazing to think of helping BTCV, thank you! Would you be okay then if I tried to get this guy I just met to go and use your funding?"

She said, "That would be perfect, I sure hope it can work!"

"Grant, this is Jimi Cook—bet you didn't think you would hear from me so soon. So, remember what I said about going on a build soon? Well, here's the deal..."

Here it is in Grant's words:

I'll never forget that lunch! It changed my life! We had a major donor in place for the India project but no non-profit and did not want to run the funding through the conventional missions channels because I wanted to put more of the money into the project. Jimi expressed that BTCV would handle that part with zero admin fees which was unheard of in terms of generosity. BTCV only had one condition: to use local volunteers whenever possible. Which we did. We did the playground and athletic field project under BTCV guidelines. I really liked using the local volunteers. I sent Jimi and Cristi a report, and their reply was, "Thanks, can you go to Malawi with us in three weeks?" What Jimi said about my wife Rachel is 100% correct, she let me go. I considered Malawi a working interview.

Three weeks later—with the help of Debbie, our travel agent, Grant's very understanding wife Rachel, and lots of big-hearted friends and family—Grant and I were standing in front of a big group of Malawians trying to figure out how we were going to get out of eating sun-dried field mice on a stick.

In Malawi, the older boys and girls catch and kill field mice. They are dried in the hot Malawian sun—*whole* (fur and all)—on sticks like shish kabobs—and then eaten—*whole* (fur and all)—as a delicacy. As such, it was a great honor and incredible gift to be offered these as their guests. The problem was we had twenty Americans and Irishman John on the team, none of whom thought this was something they wanted to try—*at all*—and were looking at me when it became apparent that receiving and eating the field mice was an expected part of the welcoming ceremony for us.

Dried field mice shish kabob

Fortunately, there were a couple songs and dances, and a welcoming speech from the village chief before the presentation of the mice for me to give to the team, which gave me time to think.

So, for my speech during the welcoming ceremony, I made sure to thank them for honoring us with the wonderful gifts and for hosting us in their village, and then said that the team would actually like to bestow this great honor on their children (who were all gathered around with eyes wide at the sight of the strange visitors and longing for the mice like our kids would be at a candy store) to signify the purpose of this partnership—for their children, the future.

It worked! And, many on the team would consider that another small miracle. The elders smiled, thanked us, and gave the mice to the children. One little girl who was about ten or eleven took hers with sheer delight, held it by the tail, and slurped it down with glee, the tail being the last thing to go, like a piece of spaghetti.

The work for this project was heavy construction on only one building and we had a pretty big team. As a result, there was a fair bit of down time for many team members, especially those who did not have much construction experience (another lesson to learn). As we always say for BTCV, *building relationships is more important than building the schools* and a lot of Changers really take this to heart. Kate was one of them. I was already impressed with her because despite her major fear of flying, she chose to fly halfway around the world with her daughter who begged her to come with her after being on the South Africa build because she thought it would be an awesome mother-daughter adventure. My respect and admiration heightened even further when I was on the roof of the library we were building, and I looked down to see Kate working with a Malawian woman who was a parent of students at the school and was trying to beautify the school grounds by doing some much-needed landscaping. The Malawian woman was just quietly working on her own, not seeking attention, not asking for help—just seeing a need and doing her part to address it. Kate did the same thing. She saw a need—the woman could use some help, the landscaping really needed done—and so she did her part to address it.

She walked from the other side of the campus where she was organizing some supplies, over to the woman, smiled (the universal language), motioned her intentions to help, and then immediately got down on her hands and knees with the Malawian woman to help her contribute to the school. It did not even take five minutes for them to be smiling, laughing, and teasing each other—in two completely different languages—as they worked side by side to change that small part of the world for the better. The campus was truly transformed by their work. It is amazing what a difference landscaping can make—even the kids noticed and appreciated it. And they built a relationship that built a global connection; *that is hand delivered hope! That is what BTCV is all about!*

I won't lie, tears were streaming down my face from that roof top—I felt so inspired, so validated, and so fulfilled—as I watched these two women change the world. That is how real change happens, that is how change is sustained, and that is what being a Changer is all about! It does not take a million dollars, heavy machinery, or a team of carpenters to accomplish our mission—it only takes a willing heart who sees a need and is willing to go, relate, empathize, and do. This is something I get to see many times on each and every build—it always works and it always inspires me to keep doing the work of hand delivered hope.

The local women would also bring the team lunch on site each day. The meals consisted of *nsima* (cornmeal porridge) and beans with the special treat of goat meat included on a couple of days. Once we finished our lunch each day, we would go play games with the kids—usually soccer, but also jump rope, tag, frisbee, relay races, and hopscotch. We often got in a round after work too before heading back to the lodge.

The second day at lunch, we were playing soccer with the kids and I noticed a young boy in a wheelchair sitting on the sidelines watching all the other kids play with obvious longing in his eyes. I asked the other kids who he was, and they said, "Sam, he is sick."

I said, "Do you think he wants to come play?"

They replied, "He can't play, he is in the chair."

I said, "Of course he can," and walked over to talk to him.

He spoke very little English but had the greatest smile in the world and we made that work for communication. He was about twelve at the time and already his legs had lost all muscle and his arms were pretty weak as well. Later, I learned this was from polio. I used a combination of words, gestures, and antics to let him know he could play if he wanted to and I would be his teammate and push his chair. He was very hesitant at first and the other kids just stood and watched initially, which did not make for much of a game, but Sam and I just went ahead and took the ball—me pushing his chair, him reaching down and pushing the ball with his hand—and scored. And, Kate jumped right in and started playing and got all the kids to play too. In a very short time it was full-on competitive soccer and I promise you, no one was giving Sam any breaks or treating him "special"—just like he wanted it and just like it should be.

Well, for better or worse, I am a very competitive person and I was quickly caught up in the game. To the point that I would get into a flat-out sprint pushing Sam's chair so he could get the ball and we could make a play. During one of these runs, the smallest player on the field, who was only five or six, jumped in front of us to try to get the ball. Well, I slammed on the brakes Fred-Flintstone-style and you can guess what happened. Sam literally went flying out of the chair like a dock-diving dog and hit the dusty Malawian ground with a thud and a skid.

Time stopped.

I was mortified, scared, and worried. Sam was face-down in the dirt, initially not moving at all.

As I rushed over to him, I could see his body shaking and I was sure that he was crying, or worse. I got to him and turned him over as the crowd of kids gathered around us. As I started to see the front of his body, I noted two scraped and bleeding knees, two scraped and bleeding elbows, a T-shirt covered in dirt, and a very dusty and dirty face ... with the biggest smile on it you have ever seen through which the laughter of pure joy was emanating.

To this day, it was one of the most beautiful—and relieving—things I have ever seen. Sam was just one of the kids—playing soccer, getting scraped up, and getting right back out there. Which he did and continued to do from that day forward. I gave him the nickname, "Sam my man," which always brought that huge smile to his face. We started letting the kids be his teammate, which made me a bit jealous, but made it sustainable. And each year we came back to Malawi, Sam and I would get in a game or two—and we always (well, almost always) won!

More importantly, I found out through the school's headmaster, our community partner, Lawrence, and Sam's family that he was an excellent student and had a dream of going to university and being a radio broadcaster. Even though the school was not set up at all to handle a student in a wheelchair, Sam found a way to make it to school every day, get up the classroom steps with the help of friends, wheel his chair to the front row, and excel! Learning about the physical hurdles he was dealing with—we immediately revised the plans for the build. We included ramps for every classroom and made sure they were wide enough and long enough to work for Sam. The coolest thing is that Sam helped us build them and worked on other parts of the project each year. He always wanted to be part of everything and wanted to earn his way in the world—and he always does.

Two more wonderful memories about Sam include the third time we came to his village for a project, Ethan (who is an American college student in a wheelchair too and you will learn more about him later) came with us. It was so amazing to see these two talk together and work together. Two amazing young people who had been struck with physical disabilities that they overcame to change their lives and the world. I cannot think of two people who inspire me more and who I am prouder to call two of my dearest friends in the world.

The second is when we came back the fourth time to his village and I went to visit him at his house. He was nineteen years old then. We looked all around the village and could not find him. I was getting worried as he definitely had highs and lows with respect to his health.

Finally, Harry (one of our amazing Malawian partners) found his older sister, whom I had never met. Harry told her who we were and that I was hoping to see Sam. She immediately burst into tears and fell into me with a strong embrace, which was not a cultural norm and in fact would be considered taboo by some. Now, I was *really* worried. But, my fears turned to unequivocal elation when Harry translated to me that Sam was at university, first in his class, and was running the campus radio station! The joy and pride I feel for Sam are unexplainable. I just keep thinking—*he made it! He did it!* And he has inspired me and so many others along the way! And, I did get to see him the next day. He looked handsome, smart, confident, and *strong*! That is the kind of strength I am after. I want to be like Sam my man!

My friend, Dusty, snapped a great photo of me pushing Sam in the very first soccer game. It is one of my favorite pictures of all time because it reminds me that everyone should be accepted and valued, that something as small as a playground soccer game can change a life, and that profound inspiration can come from the simplest things. *Just so we are clear, I am talking about what Sam my man has done for me.*

The first phase of the Malawi project was really important for us as an organization in many ways, one of which was that we learned a lot about "toxic charity" firsthand. One of the striking examples of toxic charity (TC) that we saw involved another NGO that was there at the same time who worked with widows and orphans in the village. This organization truly had hearts for these at-risk and oppressed groups, and worked hard to raise money, come visit them, and bring them gifts and supplies. It was this last component that had turned toxic in two ways.

First, the fundraising and gift-buying were not able to keep pace with the number of orphans and widows in this village and so another level of haves and have-nots had been created. The group would go into the village and gather the widows and orphans that were in the program and lead them through the village to a nearby church to give them their gifts and supplies. Everyone in town knew where they were going and saw what they had when they came back and the other widows and orphans would watch them parade through town, wondering, *why them and not me?* In addition, the widows and orphans in the program had come to expect the gifts and resources to a large degree. To me, this was not empowering or sustainable, and it struck a chord deep inside of me to always "TC-check" our mission, mechanisms, and methods to make sure we did everything we could to avoid this path.

Jimi and "Sam my man" playing soccer (and winning!)

The other example of toxic charity we experienced in Malawi came during the speeches at the celebration ceremony. The headmaster and village chief gave very similar remarks in which they first thanked us deeply and sincerely for the work we had done to help them build the library with the community. Each, though, went on very quickly to implore us, in a fairly demanding way (at least in the translation), to now provide them with water and electricity on site, even to the degree that each said the library would basically be worthless unless we came back and did those two things soon.

Several of our first-time Changers were extremely put off by this, even to the point of verbalizing it to me and some others later in terms of, "We just came halfway around the world and provided funding and labor to help them build a beautiful library, and we can't even celebrate that without them asking for more from us?" I definitely understood how these Changers felt and certainly shared that as an instinctual reaction, but also knew from a lot of reading, conversations, and experience, that this was actually not ingratitude, greed, or entitlement from the community, but rather the result of many years of toxic charity in this region.

How is this an example of toxic charity? It is because of the reason they were "asking for more" before the sun had set on the project we just completed. The reason is that many of the other NGOs, church groups, or service groups that had ever come to Makalani Village to "help" came one time, provided work, aid, or gifts that *they* thought the village needed, did everything *themselves*, did *not* determine a sustainability plan with the local leaders, and *never came back*. So, because this is how the village and school leaders perceived charity being done by "all" organizations, the mindset is that *"we only have one chance at helping our village, so we better push for everything we need now, as we will never see these people again!"* When you realize this, you understand that their requests should be respected and admired, because they are just trying to help their people as much as possible.

So, once the celebration was over and we were saying our goodbyes, we gently steered the conversation back to this point. We reminded the village and school leaders about our phased-building approach (every other year classroom refurbishment in their case), the sustainability plan we had put in place with them, and the importance of the village maintaining and improving the campus in the "off" years. As we spoke, you could see in their eyes and body language that they very much wanted to believe us, but that the years and years of organization after organization not coming through on promises to come back and to continue to work with them made them hold their trust in check. They simply bid us a warm farewell and said, "We hope and pray that we will see you again!"

Even being an eternal optimist, I had my doubts as to whether this project would continue. It just seemed like there was not enough trust or confidence in BTCV from them to motivate them to do their part.

Fast forward two years to the second build at Makalani. They had provided their annual reports, completed our Return Partner Application, and received board approval for a team of Changers to come to work with them on refurbishing the first of four classrooms in desperate need of renovation. As we got to the village to start the work (Thankfully, they didn't even offer us the dried mice shish kabobs this time), the headmaster and village chiefs were waiting for us. It was nice to see them and we exchanged warm greetings, smiles, handshakes, and hugs. I will never forget the look on the headmaster's and chief's faces as we headed to the worksite and they both simply said, "It's good to see you again!"

The implementation of this phased–building approach, starting in Malawi, has proven incredibly important to staying on mission, fostering sustainability, addressing many of our biggest mistakes, and minimizing toxic charity. A good example of this is when we came back to Makalani Village for a site evaluation and planning meeting (another vital addition to our methods) with the village chiefs, school, and community leaders after the initial phases of the project. When we got onsite, exchanged greetings, and got out our notebooks and cameras to get to work, the headmaster and one of the chiefs, who now had the biggest cat-that-ate-the-canary smiles on their faces, said, "We have something to show you first."

Oftentimes, what the local partners want to show us includes a new grandson or granddaughter, some useless piece of equipment a local politician provided to the community to buy votes, a very skinny cow the village was able to purchase, or a particularly good-looking field of maize. So, I actually was trying to think of a way to put it off politely as I really wanted to get to work. But, something in those smiles told me this was different. *And it was.*

They led us behind the classroom block and with all of the anticipation and showmanship of Bob Barker on *The Price is Right* revealing what was behind Curtain Number One, our eyes fell upon the most beautiful sight: Teachers' Housing! The community had saved money, made bricks, and worked together to build two very nice teacher housing units. They had heard us talk about the importance and benefits of teacher housing on site, took it to heart, and came through. They had done their part. They got it. They were willing to go out on a limb of trust in order to break the cycle of toxic charity. It was a big step—for them and us!

However, it is not perfect—for them and us. While the partnership has continued and all classrooms have been renovated (including wheelchair ramps) and the library is being used in many ways, toxic charity still creeps in on us from time to time. After phase two of the project, we literally left them a wad of cash so that they could get the water they wanted, and needed, hooked up—which they did right away. Major celebration! Except there was no plan for how to pay the water bill and so it was quickly shut off. We also failed to get full buy-in from each of the many village chiefs that the school serves. We did have great local leadership, buy-in from the headmaster and teachers, and support from some of the chiefs, but in a multi-village community with only one local school for all of them, it really is an "all or none" situation. We figured this out and addressed it, but it was pretty late in the game for it to result in full-on community engagement for each project and so we had to chalk this up as another valuable lesson to learn.

So, as you can see, Malawi has turned out to be a wonderful, hard, important, humbling, inspiring, challenging, and educational part of our growth and development as an organization. I don't think we would, or should, change the way it happened, as the results have been incredible overall. We were able to finish a phased, full-campus project that is sustainable and serves more than 1,000 kids with strong educational opportunities. Many of the school's graduates, including Sam my man, are able to go on to university to pursue their big hairy audacious goals and dreams. Many of our *BTCV Kids* in Malawi are excelling in their studies, getting jobs and contributing to their communities. And, a canceled vacation combined with a "quick lunch" and a phone call brought us "this guy named Grant" who has become our Director of Change and a true leader for our organization. Glenn became "OG".* And we gained an incredible Changer named "Debbie Poppins" who is known around the world for her love and generosity. Call it what you want, but to me it is another small miracle for the mission of hand delivered hope.

On the first Malawi project, Glenn wore a new pair of Oliver Goldsmith-brand designer sunglasses that had the "OG" logo on the frames. The team thought he looked really cool in them and often commented on his style and fashion sense. Dusty asked him what the "OG" stood for and without hesitating, he said, "Original Gangster," which made us all laugh hysterically because this octogenarian used that term, said it so seriously, and it painted a beautiful irony of who he was and how he treated others. So, Dusty started calling him "OG" and it quickly spread to the team and then the Malawians—and Glenn loved it! To this day, he is known around the world as OG, to the point where many of us have to think hard to remember his real name.

INDIA

When the power of love overcomes the love of power, the world will know peace.
—JIMI HENDRIX

"It took a group of foreigners to come here and show us how to love our children." That was the opening line of a heartfelt and impassioned speech delivered from a middle-aged middle-caste Indian father at the celebration ceremony after our team of Changers had worked for two weeks to help renovate a school for kids with disabilities in Kerala. What he was referring to was the way in which the team—including another group of CIS students and some Nepal-team "survivors"—had engaged and loved on the beautiful, joyful, and loving Indian students, all of whom were disabled. Most of them were dropped off at school at the beginning of the year and not often visited or brought home except at holiday breaks, if ever.

But, this father was different—he brought his severely disabled daughter to school every morning, made sure she was all set in her classroom before heading to work, and picked her up to go home every night. For the last two weeks, he observed, then talked to, then interacted with, and then trusted a team of Americans and South Africans who lit up each morning when we saw his daughter and the other students coming to class, waiting to welcome them all with big smiles and bigger hugs.

The sessions we spent with the students were more direct encounters with "pure joy" for me and this team. We sang songs with them, did morning stretches and exercises with them, worked on crafts with them, played games with them, read books with them, and listened to their stories, lists of favorite things, wishes, goals, and dreams. We enjoyed it so much. We would all get lost in the moment, turn into little kids ourselves, belly-laugh, giggle, cheer, forget to use our "inside voices," and completely lose track of time during each session with these incredible kids. We learned most of these kids' stories from the teachers, but we learned this father's story directly from him. It was hard for him. Hard to learn that his child was born with a severe disability. Hard to accept the stigma from family, friends, outsiders, and the culture. Hard to find a school his daughter could go to. Hard to afford the care, boarding, transportation, and education his daughter needed. Hard to be there for his daughter each and every day, still hold down a full-time job, and still care for his wife and two other children. Hard to not constantly ask, "Why?"

So, when he stood in front of the team he had learned to trust over the two weeks we were there, facing all the other parents, and especially the upper-caste school and community dignitaries, many of whom only wanted to be seen at the "prestigious" celebration, it is no wonder that he was trembling. But, as he began to speak, I realized that he was not trembling with fear. Instead, he was trembling with passion. This father wanted to be heard. He wanted to use his voice to start a ripple that could start to change an entire culture. So as he trembled, he spoke with perfect clarity, purpose, and passion. He held his head high as he delivered each word, each clearly coming straight from his heart:

It took a group of foreigners to come here and show us how to love our children. Many of our children are abandoned at this school. We are ashamed of them. We do not count them as our children. We do not value them or even accept them—our own children. Indian children. But, these people who come under the banner of one of our own countrymen—a man we revere and idolize—Mahatma Gandhi, who told us all to be the change we wish to see in the world, have done exactly that. The change they want to see is all children, boys and girls, whole and not whole, be loved, valued and given the gift of education—in whatever form that may be. They have done exactly that. That are showing us what Gandhi meant. They have showed us how to love our own children. Our Indian children. Our precious children. I beg you to listen afresh to Gandhi's words. I beg you to follow these foreigners' example. I beg you to love your children.

There was not even a whisper to be heard and barely a dry eye in the house. He made his point—even more, I believe he started a ripple, and it was a very important and powerful ripple that I have tried to spread throughout the world for him. *I hope that you will too. I beg you to be part of this ripple effect that a warm-hearted, kind, and impassioned Indian father started in a small school in Southern India. I beg you to listen afresh to Gandhi's words. I beg you to love your children. And, I beg you to consider every child in the world...yours!*

A few years later in the opposite end of India, an equally powerful point was made that I have also tried to spread throughout the world. This time though, the point was not made through words, but through actions. In a tiny rural community in Bihar where we had just helped complete phase one of a new construction project, we sat on the decorated guest platform anxiously waiting for the crowd to arrive for the dedication of the school.

This was to be more than just a celebration of the work that was done and the opportunity for education that came out of it. This ceremony would help determine whether the school would be successful or not because the leaders of each sect of the community would have to give it their blessings and endorsement for parents to send their kids to this school. This was a major hinge point in this community because there were other schools in the area that were either government schools or religious schools, which had been around a long time. This new school was, *well new*, and it had an apparent outside influence, which is always viewed with skepticism and caution, especially when the outside influence appears to be primarily American.

This school did have a chance though, because the other schools were either run-down, poorly run, had no funding, or were not open to the entire community. But, if one or more of the community leaders did not support it, the school would likely fail. That is daunting enough, but add on to it that the community leaders were Christian, Hindu, or Muslim, and from different castes, and we were looking at needing another miracle for this school to survive, even before it really got started.

This had been a unique build for many reasons already. Debbie—*yes that Debbie and yes her first build was with Grant (how cool is that?)*—finally got to go on a build, and man, were we glad. Debbie is one of those people that just brings light to a room and joy and courage to those she is with. All of these attributes are incredibly helpful and important on school building projects in the developing world—especially to a team of "first world" volunteers who are out of their element and just trying to figure out this whole "Changer thing."

She also brings a lot of other things to a project—like everything you needed but forgot to pack. On every project Debbie has been on, Changers, new and veteran, would casually mention something they wish they had, ask the team if they could borrow *x, y, or z*, or tell the team leader about something they forgot and really needed. Debbie would say *"just a moment"* and go to her room, get her bag, and reach into it. Like magic, her hand would search around the bag for a bit, seemingly going to depths that did not physically match the geometry of the bag and pull out exactly what we needed, wanted, or asked for (including peanut butter M&Ms for Grant and me). It reminded everyone of Mary Poppins and her magic carpet bag and so Debbie quickly got the nickname, "Debbie Poppins." It fit and to this day, I sometimes forget her real last name. Builds with Debbie Poppins are extra special and she has also volunteered her time as our Executive Coordinator of Change in her retirement.

This project was also unique because we had to navigate and address local politics much more extensively than ever before. Mostly Grant and I, but sometimes the whole team, would be asked (actually really told) to come meet with a local leader, be it religious, political, or business, for tea, lunch, or dinner, to pay our respects and explain our purpose to them. This was problematic for several reasons.

First, when I am on a build, I want to work hard to get the project done well and on time, and really don't like to be interrupted or take time away from the work. Second, I am not big on "playing the political game" and much prefer working, talking, and interacting with the kids, teachers, parents, and grandparents who are the "boots on the ground" people we are partnering with. Third, I was always a bit worried about what I would be asked to drink or eat. And, lastly, I am pretty blunt and straightforward when it comes to my beliefs and the BTCV purpose and mission, so I was worried I could offend one or more of these leaders and jeopardize the project, especially since I was really unfamiliar with Indian culture and politics.

Fortunately, Grant was fairly familiar with Indian culture and politics and was savvy enough to navigate these treacherous waters. When we would be summoned to a meeting while in the middle of digging, mixing mortar or laying bricks and I would roll my eyes and begrudgingly hand my tools to another Changer or community worker, Grant would hand me a clean shirt on our way to the *tuk tuk* (motorized rickshaw) and brief me on who the meeting was with, what their concerns were, why they cared, what they wanted, what to say and what not to say. Picture the press secretary briefing the president on the way to a major summit, except that we were in the middle of remote northern India wearing shorts and work boots getting into a *tuk tuk* to go sit on the rustic front porch of hand-hewn village homes of people who look and dress very differently from us to drink tea from unmatched cups from who-knows-where.

These meetings were all incredibly different and yet remarkably the same. And, the hope for a better future is the one thing that can immediately create common ground no matter what the other variables are, and the opportunity for education as the premise for that hope is powerful. This commonality, and the fact that Grant did a great job prepping me, and more importantly, in navigating all of these meetings, resulted in all of them ending with big smiles, warm handshakes, promises and commitments to the school.

This takes us back to the celebration ceremony platform. Our anxiety grew and grew as many of the students started to show up, but none of the leaders had been seen or heard from yet. Then the Christian leader whose organization coordinates the operations of the school showed up on the back of a motorcycle. *Progress.* We greeted him, showed him to the platform, and made small talk while we waited. Then, the Hindu leader who provided the land to the partner organization and lives across the street from the school arrived on foot. Then, the Muslim leader whose family handles all of the masonry work at the school pulled up in a *tuk tuk*. Finally, a shiny SUV drove in through the school gate at a bit too fast rate of speed and pulled all the way up to the back of the gathering crowd. This made us a bit more nervous as we were not sure if this was going to be the start or the finish of our planned ceremony. Our apprehension grew as a very well-dressed man who was significantly taller and broader than the local villagers stepped out of the car. I looked at Grant and then the other dignitaries—all shared the same questioning look. But then we recognized the man as one of the key politicians we had tea with during our tour promoting the school to gain full buy-in. This was an added bonus and a great sign, and to top it off, he had brought his young daughter to the ceremony. Typically, a guy like this would send a lower level politician, or even just an aide, to a village ceremony like this. But, this was different. He was here himself with his daughter to be part of this village-school dedication. This is what we could consider a "caste-shattering event."

Do you believe in miracles? I do!

All these leaders sat next to each other on the platform and not only endorsed the school, but demanded that their communities all support this school strongly. This ceremony and this school also brought political parties together. Indian National Congress and Bharatiya Janata Party members, who can be vehemently and violently separated on every other aspect of life, came together for education. And, they even allowed and sat attentively when a female student and a mother from the community spoke passionately about the importance of girls' education and opportunities for women and when I praised the courage and leadership a young Pakistani girl—Malala Yousafzai for standing up to Al-Qaeda in support of girls' education, for which she almost lost her life. To even allow a woman and a girl to speak was a major victory. To let them passionately implore the now-diverse audience to provide the same educational opportunities to all community members—boys, girls, low-caste, middle-caste, high-caste, Christian, Muslim, Hindu, India National Congress, Bharatiya Janata Party—was the coup d'état. To allow an outsider, an American, to tout a Pakistani girl as a hero and an example to be followed and applaud my words was unimaginable... *you might even say miraculous!*

An Indian mother speaking passionately about girls' education at the celebration ceremony

But, the real miracle is that this was not just "for show" and did not end when the celebratory tea and biscuits were gone. This school is completely self-sustainable and has grown tremendously—physically with four more phases in partnership with BTCV, in student and teacher numbers, in resources, in academic success, and in a work of togetherness for their kids' futures.

The message those leaders and this community sent that day is that the power of education can overcome deep-seated beliefs, stereotypes, and stigmas. The desire for a better future for your children and grandchildren is a powerful force that can make even the most guarded and most cynical reconsider their views and open their hearts to a willingness to share, learn, and engage. In short, education—and the hope it brings—can change everything!

As you can see, India has been eye-opening and perspective-changing in many ways. We have learned so much as individuals and as an organization. We were starting to consistently apply our lessons learned and see them come to fruition—creating relationships, ensuring buy-in, spending time interviewing parents, teachers, students, and local leaders through a focused school-needs analysis process before starting the work—resulting in engaged communities and sustainable and impactful outcomes.

But, sticking strongly to our mission also meant "firing" some volunteers. *Man, you talk about tough.* These were among the most painful things we have ever had to do in BTCV, but also among the most important. A person who is not on board with both the mission and methods can completely derail a project, and even destroy an organization. We made some very difficult phone calls, before and after builds, to respectfully but firmly explain why we had to not allow a volunteer to volunteer with us. It definitely took me back to that phone call with Mr. Brian Anderson, and gave me more respect for that process and more understanding of why he didn't tell us right away if we could go on that project and be part of that team. Growing up is hard—as an individual or as an organization—and we definitely were going through some tough growing pains (with more to come), but seeing the results of the hard work of staying on mission kept us going...and growing.

The India builds also had their own sets of unique challenges.

Cutting bamboo in a human-waste field.

Being chased down on the highway by a *tuk tuk* gang because we were not using their drivers.

Traveling hours and hours in harrowing traffic on four-lane highways where traffic goes in both directions in all four lanes, large rice harvests are drying in middle of the highway, and the rules of the road are that the biggest and bravest win.

Traveling hours and hours in a standing-room only train where people, including Changers, were packed in so tight that the only place to "sit" was up in the luggage racks.

Numerous strikes and blockades that we had to talk our way out of or around.

Being held at immigration many times because our passports or visas "were not proper," which really meant we needed to bribe them and were too naïve to realize it.

But I can say with confidence that the two life-changing, caste-shattering events described above are things that all who experienced them will hold in their hearts forever and treasure as true miracles that they got to witness first hand. And, I know we are all working hard to apply these great truths and spread them around the world. *I hope you will too!*

KENYA

You build on failure. You use it as a stepping stone. Close the door on the past. You don't try to forget the mistakes, but you don't dwell on it. You don't let it have any of your energy, or any of your time, or any of your space.

—Johnny Cash

Okay, now we really do have this school building thing figured out—that was definitely the thought and feeling we all shared as we continued to take on new projects in new parts of the world with new communities. In just our first seven years of education focused development aid, we had completed sixteen projects in Rwanda, Cambodia, Papua New Guinea, South Africa, Viet Nam, Nepal, Ethiopia, Malawi, Sri Lanka, India, Thailand and Tanzania.

Then, as I was walking through Chicago O'Hare to catch a flight, my cell phone rang. It was an international number, which is not rare for me, but was one I didn't recognize nor was I expecting. I almost didn't take it, thinking that it was probably one of my friends wanting to ask about a case or see if I could come do a talk at a conference. But, then I remembered that we had a BTCV team on the ground in Kenya, and figured that I better make sure.

"Jimi, it's Grant. We have a big problem."

What I was about to find out stopped me in my tracks.

Here is the summary of the crazy, humbling, lesson-learning story in Grant's own words with some color commentary from me.

I have spent the last six years trying to forget Kenya. I had been to Malawi with BTCV prior to this. Malawi was not perfect but it was a great team, great leaders and a good project. Malawi had set the bar. This was my first trip leading a team for BTCV. Other than one person on the team, everyone who volunteered to go with me was a close personal friend or family member. At this time, BTCV did not have a board of directors; it was just the four original co-founders with huge hearts and a lot of raw passion to change the world. I wanted to be part of that and I wanted to prove to them I could build schools for this organization.

At this point in BTCV's history, the application process for projects was a few brief questions to whoever contacted us to "get our help for their school" and then an ongoing email conversation to sort out the details of the project. The project for Kenya had been presented to us by a woman in Oregon who had been to Kenya and worked with another NGO. The Oregon woman had funded the construction of a children's home, which was a beautiful complex built for 150 orphans. Her contact was a man named Okeyo Bob Nyangige. She told us that he was a trustworthy person and that she had worked with him before.

There were red flags prior to the trip. Bob had sent us photos of kids telling us they were orphans (remember the home was built for 150 orphans, but the photos showed only about forty kids). He also sent a photo of the home staff of about ten adults—not with the kids and not at the home. But, I was blinded by my desire to push forward and make the project a reality and ignored all the red flags

JC: Grant was not alone in missing these red flags and I was definitely the main one driving the "just do it, send the money, take the team, it will be fine" mentality on this one.

I still imagined all of these students and the staff joining hands and singing Kumba-yah everyday as they passed bricks together with our team to help build their new school on the children's home campus. Bob told us that a school could be built for $10,000 in US dollars. So, I convinced my friends and family to sign on, give their money, and raise money from their friends and family for this school. I purchased the group's flights online myself instead of using a travel agent which saved us some money but I would never do it again. Now we have a travel agent. And now we require pre-payment.

Lesson Learned: Whenever possible use experts and don't believe yourself to be capable of doing everything well!

A few weeks before the trip I had a call with the Oregon woman. During that call she admitted to me that when she was working with Bob, government officials showed up and forced her to leave the country. She said she was "terrified." That was information that probably would have been helpful prior to the purchase of flights. I called Jimi and told him I thought everything would still be okay. I was pushing forward rather than thinking clearly. Jimi believed in me and allowed me to continue the project and take the team after I assured him it would be okay.

Lesson Learned: Pay attention to red flags! At this point it would have been better to refund the team's money and cut our losses until we did more research.

Well, the team arrived in Kenya with no issues and I was just praying that this guy, Bob, was going to show up with a vehicle to pick us up. I had never actually met him, another mistake. We got our bags and walked outside the Nairobi airport. It took a few minutes (I was a little worried in my head) then these two Kenyan guys approached us. Bob was there with his friend, Bennett. They showed us to a nice big van and drove us to a hotel. Everything was going fine.

We stayed overnight in a hotel in Nairobi. Now here is probably the biggest lesson, so lean in. That first night, I gave Bob all the team's money: for construction, for food, lodging, transport—everything. I can guess what every reader is thinking, "How stupid!" You are correct, it was stupid. Before BTCV, I had been learning about managing developing world mission projects from my Dad and our right-hand man in India, Gulshan, on the streets of rural West Bengal, India. In Kenya, I basically threw everything I had learned out the window. I was pushing forward with raw passion for the mission, blind trust for my new project partner, and love for the kids.

Additionally, I have to admit, I was pushing forward for myself. Some of it was arrogance and pride telling myself, I can do this, I can handle it, I've got this, I have thought of everything. I had brought some emergency money and kept that in my belt, which was one of the last intelligent things I would do in Kenya.

JC: This is also the BTCV leadership model that Grant was exposed to as it is certainly the way we were still doing BTCV as co-founders—raw passion, unchecked trust, blind faith, and very authentic but sometimes toxic love for kids and communities. This book hopefully shows how we kept the passion, trust, faith and love, but refined, matured, and focused the mission and the methods.

Lesson Learned: Don't give all the money up front to new project partners.

Lesson Learned: Always have enough emergency cash with you.

The next day Bob showed up at the Nairobi hotel with his teenage son (who had a brand-new iPod?) and Bennett. We got in the van and took off. All was well! But then a school site that was supposed to be four hours from Nairobi was six, maybe eight hours away. We got to the end of the paved roads at four hours and then started a brutal hours-long drive on some of the worst dirt pothole-ridden roads I have ever traveled. I would venture to say that for some segments you could not even call it a true road.

Team members were getting car sick, and asking "How much farther is it?"

This was the first sign of what was coming on this project—and it wasn't good.

Before BTCV, it was just me, my Dad, Gulshan and a Jeep, train, or motorcycle in India. No expectations, no problems for two or three guys. But, this was a big problem for a group of unseasoned travelers who volunteered to help orphans in Africa and were not prepared for any of this.

We eventually arrived in the small town where the school was to be built. Bob took us to our accommodations, a rough brick courtyard type structure with no windows. It looked more like a small prison yard on the inside. It had twelve-foot-high brick walls. It had a large steel door (remember the door for later). There were several rooms with metal bar doors, I mean this looked like a prison—a rustic African prison in the middle of nowhere at that. At the back was the bathroom. A stand-over-pit toilet next to an open bathing room for bucket baths. Again, none of this would have been a problem for two guys in a Jeep (me and Gulshan). This was a big problem for a group of women and men who did not bring camping gear and were not at all expecting this.

Lesson Learned: For new projects, send a small team in advance, do a site visit, meet the local partner, make the journey, see the accommodations, meet the community, see the kids, see the building site, understand the logistics—so that you can prepare your team and create appropriate expectations and manage those expectations honestly.

Believe it or not, everyone was still a good sport about it and really the overall excitement of the project overshadowed the living conditions, at least for the first couple of days. Bob had asked for $40 per night per person to include meals. What we know now is that lodging like this would cost more like $3 per night *and basic meals would be more like $10 per day. Bob was pocketing our money. But what could we do now? He had it all and we were a full day's drive from Nairobi. On-site red flag number one.*

Lesson Learned: Always have a backup plan for when that first transport, food and lodging plan falls through. Because in the developing world, Plan A has a fifty-fifty chance of working even if you do all your "homework" in advance.

The next day the team was excited to get out to the school and get to work. The van we rode to the school in had left and Bob had hired a small car with a driver. Okay, no problem, we can go in two groups everywhere, it will be fine. It was not fine. You see, that little car could not hold an entire team, it could not haul materials, and it had a driver with a mind of his own.

We have learned that hired drivers will sometimes disappear for hours with the team's vehicle. What are they doing? Sometimes they are out burning your gas and making money as a local cab. Sometimes they are showing off the car to friends. So, I had to make some clear rules with Bob and the driver. By day three, I would get out of that little car and put my hand out. The driver knew to put the keys in my hand so that he could not leave. The driver also knew by then that when he took half the team somewhere he had to come straight back for the other half—yes, this was a real problem.

Lesson Learned: Evaluate the transport long before bringing a team. When possible just do the local driving yourself. Always control the vehicles.

Now back to the school. Bob said the construction had already started. He had assured us in his emails that he was qualified to manage the project, including construction, so we did not hire a contractor. Another bad move.

JC: I am glad Grant started using "us" and "we" here because I was definitely involved in these emails and decisions.

Lesson Learned: Always hire local professionals to manage the project with you.

We drove to the site the first day—about fifteen minutes down a dirt road—and there was a half-built, two-classroom building there. I was relieved! We got out of the vehicle and started checking out the area. Everyone was excited! After about thirty minutes of checking things out, I said, "All right, let's get to work."

That's when it happened. I looked around the building. I looked in the back. I looked inside. No construction materials. There were a few boards and a few bricks and one lone worker tinkering with the masonry.

Where was the roofing lumber?

Where was the concrete?

Where was the metal roofing?

Where were the windows and doors?

Where were the soccer goals we were going to set?

Bob, with a shaky laugh and smile, said with a wave that he would go get those things now and be right back. I believed him. (Stupid). On-site red flag number two.

Bob hopped in the one car we had and drove off. We did not see Bob again for four hours.

We were just out there. No tools, no supplies, no local contact, and no shade other than the wall of the half-built building.

The team members, aka my friends and family, started asking me questions. I gave them some fluff about how "time does not matter in these countries," "it's just the way life is here," "we need to be culturally understanding." Inside I was fuming. We had no water and no food.

So I asked my best friend of twenty years, Eric Welton, to go find bottled water back at the market. Eric, who gave us his hard-earned overtime checks from his job as a mechanic to join this project, had never been outside the US before, but he was a biker dude and if anyone could handle anything it was Eric.

So, Eric took off alone on foot to find water in the market that was a couple miles back. An hour later, he came back over the hill on the back of a motorcycle with a case of water. He gave the driver some coins and a fist bump (yes, this really happened) and walked over with the water to a thirsty team. A small victory!

Today I realize that this could have been a catastrophic tragedy. You see I sent Eric out alone in a place we don't know with people we don't know. The worst could have happened.

Lesson Learned: No one goes anywhere alone.

When Bob did get back, he had two women with him. They brought the team lunch. But no tools or construction materials. There was no real lunch set-up or plan, so the team grabbed plates and sat against the wall of the school eating rice and beans.

I asked Bob where everything was and he said that he would go get it now. I said, "No! We will go together." We hopped in the car and drove off. I am sure the team was thrilled to see me drive off with Bob.

We got to the market and Bob was clearly lost. He went to one kiosk-type structure and started negotiating for one single hammer made out of a bent chunk of metal. Was he nuts? I was like "Bob, where is everything? Where are the supplies, where are the tools? Where are the orphans? Where is the Children's Home?"

Bob finally confessed. There was a bad turn of events just prior to the team's arrival. He had wrecked another person's car and some of BTCV's money was needed to pay that debt.

"What? What does your car wreck have to do with anything?"

The answer didn't matter though because the reality was we were stuck. We went back to the site. I gave my brother-in-law, Dan, who I had also convinced to give us money and join us for the nightmare, a hand saw we had brought from the US with us (at the time BTCV did not travel with full tool boxes). We sawed up the few boards that were on site and were able to make a couple trusses. There was not enough lumber for all the trusses needed. That was it for the day.

We went back to the accommodations and of course there was none of the drinking water Bob said he would get. I took off on foot because Bob had left, again, with the car. I found bottled water and carried it back to the group. Every day, I would leave in the morning on foot to get our water on foot because it was never taken care of by Bob or his "team."

Lesson Learned: Always know where water is and always have enough for your team. Having more than enough drinking water actually gives people a sense of security. When it's two guys in the bush it's easy to handle that type of thing. When you have ten people it becomes more difficult, and when you have twenty it's a full-time job. Water matters!

The next day. "Bob, where is the Children's Home?" He said it was within walking distance and it was.

It was a beautiful set of buildings with a kitchen and dorms and space. I asked why we weren't staying there? Then I realized it was abandoned. You see the Oregon woman had given money to build the building. The purchase of the land, however, was the issue. The owner took the land back somehow after the buildings were completed, and of course, he got to keep the buildings built on his land.

What we would later learn is that the orphanage was at one time (for a very short period) full of kids and had a full staff. It was short-lived as there was no business plan and no method for sustainability, so it closed. Bob and the Oregon woman failed to mention this to us ... the Oregon woman later confessed to me that she hoped BTCV would take over the whole thing and make it work; that's why she withheld the information.

Lesson Learned: Make sure the land ownership is clear and documented and the community has a viable sustainability plan.

Lesson Learned: Believe the best about the project, but do your due diligence for the worst-case scenario.

"Bob, where are the orphans now? Remember the photo with forty kids?"

Bob took us to a house where there were about ten kids living with a woman. These were the orphans that we were building a school for: miles from their location, no teachers, no school funding. This was not going to work at all.

At this point, I felt I had to tell Jimi what was happening. I contacted him by phone and told him everything. He was like "Man, that's terrible!" Then, he first gave me words of encouragement that were greatly needed.

And, then he told me something that turned my thinking around and actually gave me some real comfort. He said, "Grant, do whatever you have to do to take care of that team."

I was still really concerned with the team's experience and building the school and not wasting my friends' and family's money. That statement from Jimi gave me the direction of thinking that I needed. At this point the project was shot. I needed to take care of the team.

JC: This was the "Chicago-airport Kenya call" for me. On my end, it was:

"Jimi, it's Grant. We have a big problem."

And then a shortened but very intense version of the story above was relayed to me through a less-than-perfect cell phone connection.

"Grant, is everyone all right? Are you safe?"

"Yes, we are safe. Some people are pretty freaked out, but we are fine. I need to figure out how to get this project back on track though—we have to do this right for BTCV."

This is one of the many things that I love about Grant and why he has helped make BTCV what it has become. He has the highest integrity and utmost accountability to our mission, our donors, and our volunteers. But, in this instance, accountability of intended use of funds was trumped by accountability to safety and overall mission. So, I did encourage him and I did tell him to do whatever he had to in order to take care of the team. We had both failed to see the red flags, we made huge mistakes, we trusted another good-heart-bad-methods individual who ended up doing very toxic charity, and we gave our faith and money to a crook instead of a partner. The project was a bust. It was time to cut our losses, take care of the team, and get everyone home safe. Then we could reassess, do damage control, and try to learn *all* the lessons we had to—quickly and well.

I told Grant that if he needed more money, I would get it to him. "Just take care of that team, Brother! And take care of yourself!"

Grant again: *That night I called Bob. No answer. Called again. No answer. Called again. Finally, he answered.*

It's the middle of the night, I am sitting with my friend Eric next to me. And I am demanding to know what is happening?

Bob says for me to come out to the school. Remember it's the middle of the night in Africa. One thing I did know was driving around after dark in this part of the world is a great way to disappear forever. I looked at Eric, he shook his head "no." We went back to the accommodations. If Eric had not been there, I think I would have gone and who knows what would have happened that night. Bob just never came through on this project. The next day Bob just left. He did not come back for a couple days.

My friends were confused and rightfully so. This was not in the plan. A breaking point happened for my good friend from church who I had convinced to raise money from his family, give his own money, and bring his wife—he finally snapped. He looked right at me and said with an aggressive voice, "You need to tell us what is going on! (I could tell he felt unsafe and I had no defense. He was right. To this day, I have not been able to restore that relationship.)

Lesson Learned: Don't beat around the bush and try to fool your team. If people feel afraid, all bets are off. Take them someplace they feel safe at all costs.

When Bob came back I was like, "Man where have you been, what is happening?" Bob said, "I was only gone a few days, I had family business." He said it like there was no issue – why should I be upset?

I learned a lot more about African "timelessness" on this project than I wanted to—at least one African's timelessness. I learned that this is how Bob would stall for time. You see, Bob had no plan. No experience with teams. His original plan went out the window when he spent the money we gave him on his debts rather than the school. My best guess is that he thought he could just stall for time until we had to leave the country, which actually ended up being correct.

Lesson Learned: Make timelines and schedules for the application, planning, and building phases of the project. Discuss and agree on them and use them to evaluate projects and partners.

Every night my sweet wife, Rachel, who I had convinced to join us, tried to comfort me. I was defeated. It was humiliating. I even lashed out at her one night saying how she did not understand anything. She understood everything because she was watching it unfold in real time. Fortunately, a few years later I got to take her to see a real BTCV success story in India.

Lesson Learned: Don't be a jerk just because things are not going your way. Suck it up, boot up, and be a leader!

Maybe Bob did have some shred of conscience because when he got back, he said we were going to have dinner at a friend's house. Great, I thought. What trap or con is this?

We headed to the edge of town, and on the way, there were two men standing in the road in flip-flops, military fatigue pants and t-shirts, holding rifles. They were the local militia and charged "50 bob" (five dollars) to pass. It was a customary charge and obviously much higher for outsiders. This was a little unnerving for some team members and I thought that might be the final straw and the team might just start walking to the airport right then and there.

But just then, as we drove over a hill on the dirt road, I saw it. A beautiful Catholic mission with vineyards, buildings, and even a clean, well-kept hospital. It was like an oasis in the middle of nowhere. Bob's friend at this mission was the same woman who had been bringing us meals. She had an apartment on site because she worked at the mission hospital. There was electricity, running water, a clean flush-toilet. In her apartment, I also noticed a brand-new flat screen TV in use with the open box next to it.

This is where we learned that sometimes "local volunteers" means your contact is paying everyone to get them to participate, and there really are no true volunteers. They want the project and the money that comes with it, and they will tell you whatever they think you need to hear to get that money and get that school. We don't like to believe this but we have to accept it as reality in some situations. We have encountered this again on projects and have come to learn that, in the end, our mission is not to ensure that local volunteers are really volunteering. Our mission is to create sustainable educational opportunities for deserving kids, and that community buy-in can happen without all participants being true volunteers. But, the community involvement has to be genuine, sincere, and sustainable. In Kenya, it was not.

Another good thing did happen that night at the mission though. I met one of the priests. He was a great guy and showed me around. They had a school, a vocational program, and missionary lodging! Why weren't we partnered with this guy? We walked into a building that had individual rooms with their own bathrooms and flushing toilets! He told me privately that he didn't even know Bob.

I told Bob that the team would be moving here to the mission for lodging. The priest and I had made a deal for rooms and I had paid him with emergency money in advance while we were alone. Bob said we could not move because he had made a deal with the other guest house (a very profitable deal for Bob). I said "Nope, we are moving." I really needed to do something to make the team feel safe and get things at least somewhat under control until we could get headed back home.

The next day we were packing our bags at the old guest house. Fortunately, part of the team including my friend who rightfully felt unsafe, was out by the lake and not present for this part. While the rest of us were packing, the owner of the guesthouse showed up with a bigger guy (the muscle) and began arguing with Bob in another language. Then it happened. The bigger guy walked over to the large steel door, slammed it shut, and slapped a lock on it from the inside.

My first instinct was to attack the guy and beat him unconscious. I was very certain I could do it at this point. Fortunately I did not attempt that. Bob continued arguing with the man. Tension was rising and then my wife's best friend from college, Trisha, a true Changer, who was with us as all of this was happening, went into her room and came out with a chair and magazine. She sat down in the sun right there amidst all of it and began to read as if to say, "Let me know how this goes." The girl is cool, collected, and fearless.

I walked over to Bob, put my hands up, and asked how much money the guy wanted. It wasn't much, so we paid him and left.

I sent the first group to the mission and stayed with the rest of the team. I learned here that team leaders in every situation are first in and last out. I waited to be the last one to leave that hell hole. This goes for crazy emergencies like this and flights to and from countries.

Lesson Learned: Keep your cool and don't get physical unless it is an absolute last resort. Most of the issues you will face in the developing world are questions of cash: how much to fix this now? It is a reality we have to understand.

The Catholic mission was a game changer in terms of safety, comfort, and assurance. Another positive was that Eric, the biker dude who got us water, is also the best mechanic on the planet. The mission had a caterpillar machine they could not use because the bucket would not lift. Eric went to town, bought a tube of some goo he said "wasn't the right stuff, but he could work with it." Then, he made temporary gaskets for the hydraulic hoses and basically fixed the machine. He also fixed the pump that brought water up from the lake to the kitchen. The rest of the team was also able to engage in some meaningful work around the mission. The priest was so happy that he organized a big dinner for the team with wonderful food—another game changer!

Lesson Learned: It's really important to have people with big hearts on projects and it's also really important to have people with specific skill sets (like mechanics) on projects in the developing world. Eric was invaluable out in the bush.

While the new accommodations were a game changer for avoiding a complete disaster and revolt, the team's morale was already shot. The team's trust for me was long gone. My friends, my wife, my brother-in-law, and probably the worst for me, my father, had just spent a week watching me fail and be humiliated hour after hour. Then, my dad came to me and said, "Hey son, I got a car and am going up north to meet a guy." I was like, "What? You just hired a car? Dad, you can't leave now."

Dad was like, "Nah son, you got this." And he just left. Dad is an on-the-job-training kind of guy and an old-school businessman. Part of me thinks he did it to help me grow and part of me thinks he did it because he was like "yeah, this is Africa, what did the kid expect."

I called Jimi again and told him I thought we should leave early. Jimi gave me words of encouragement, because what else can you do from the other side of the planet, and he said again, "Grant, do whatever you need to do to take care of that team."

There was nothing more we could do. The construction materials never came and to this day, the building was never finished.

When we left for our scheduled safari, that was the last time we ever saw Bob. The safari was good for the team as it took their minds off the school disaster and signaled to them that we were headed home alive. For me, by this time, I was exhausted and humiliated. I just wanted to crawl under a rock and go home. After the safari, we headed back to Nairobi. Finally, this nightmare was about to end—or not.

When we reached the city limits, Bennett and the driver begin arguing. Bennett looked concerned. I asked him what was up. He said it was nothing. It did not look like a nothing argument. It's in another language so I have no idea what they are saying. They are just yelling at each other. The team, of course, noticed.

Then, we pulled into the Central Nairobi Police Station.

"What are we doing here?" I asked

No answer.

We pull into a gated area which was the vehicle impound. The driver goes inside and Bennett goes inside. It is getting dark outside. We have four hours until our flight. I sit there for a few minutes. The team is visibly concerned.

Finally, I get out of the bus and I walk inside the police station. It looks like something out of the movies. Low light, chipped light blue paint, cigarette smoke, chattering in another language. The driver is talking to a man wearing a police uniform that is clearly too big for him. Bennett is standing there nervously looking at me.

"What is the deal? Take us to the airport!" I said.

The driver says something to Bennett. Bennett tells me that Bob did not pay the driver for the trip home and they are not going to take us to the airport until they get the money. I look at a policeman behind a desk who is reading a paper smoking a cigarette. He looks like the guy in charge. I walk over and say "You can't hold a bus full of Americans here. I am gonna' call the embassy!" He looks up from his paper, puffs his cigarette, and looks back down at his paper and says nothing.

That's when it hits me. We are about to miss our flights. And, these guys know it. Jimi had already told me to "do whatever I needed to do to take care of this team."

I went back out to the bus. Bennett followed me. As we walked up to the bus, I saw a line of cabs. I made a backup plan in my head that we would go to the cabs and pay them to take us to the airport.

The driver came out of the station behind us and another man walked up out of nowhere. He was the owner of the bus. A short, flashy well-groomed guy. We stood behind the bus and he said.

"You gotta' pay if you want to go to the airport. You gotta' pay $500." I learned right then and there that once any locals with bad motives know you're heading to the airport, they have two things on you. One, they know you're on a schedule for flights that cost a lot of money. Two, this is their last chance to get their hands on your money.

I don't remember everything that went on from there honestly as it all happened really fast. I did what Gulshan would have done. I said, "I'll give you $300 here and $200 at the airport." He said "Let's go."

We got in the bus and I purposefully sat directly behind the driver. I was done with all of this. If that driver had turned off the main road before the airport, then I was going to do whatever I needed to do to get this team safely out of Kenya.

Thank God we shortly arrived at the airport. I paid the man the rest of the bribe money just as my dad was walking up to the group smiling as though it was just another day at the office.

Bennett said to me, "Grant, I have not been paid by Bob either."

I said, "But you're a volunteer?"

He said, "Yes! I am a volunteer! But Bob agreed to pay me!"

My dad handed Bennett a package of cookies, smiled, and walked inside.

I said, "That's between you and Bob." We took our bags and walked into the airport.

My dad could tell I was defeated. He said, "Son, I have literally dealt with everything you have on this trip. The difference is you got to experience it all in less than two weeks and I had it happen to me over a twenty-year period. You learned a lot."

Not comforting at all, but true. I learned a lot.

I know I called and texted with Jimi the entire time. It was up and down. It's a blur. Through it all he encouraged me and kept me sane. I don't remember caring about other people's money as much as getting these people out of Kenya. I have spent the last six years trying to forget Kenya, so I could be wrong. I do remember telling Jimi to make sure there was enough money in the bank to purchase new flights for the team because BTCV was so hand-to-mouth that I was worried about enough money to escape Kenya.

Through the entire experience, in phone calls and text messages, Jimi was completely comforting and reassuring to me that I could handle this. Not many leaders of leaders would have kept their cool in the way Jimi did, especially knowing about the gravity of the situation. His trust and words of encouragement definitely helped me make better decisions and get my thinking right. Team first.

On the flight home, I was uncertain about BTCV. Kenya cost me a lot personally; if there were a ranking system I would put it in the top three for most humiliating and humbling experiences of my life. Obviously, BTCV kept me around and we did change the way we operate from the lessons we learned in Kenya and Nepal and the others.

In fact, I got right back on the horse. Going to Papua New Guinea a few months later was both healing and continued to be eye opening. Being on the ground there for thirty days straight versus two weeks allowed me to see what was genuine in PNG and what was fabricated for the sake of BTCV donors and volunteers. At first, some of this knowledge discouraged me. But, what I have learned through these things is that God is trying to show us what to be less concerned with and what our real mission is. Our real mission is not making project partners fulfill our desires. Our real mission is building schools for students with little or no opportunity to provide the educational opportunities that they truly deserve.

JC: Grant did call me again from the police station.

Jimi, now the team is on a bus in a police impound yard on the way to the airport and they are saying that they are going to hold us here until we give them $500. We are going to miss our flights if we have to stay much longer. I have a plan, but I just need to make sure we have enough money in the BTCV account to buy flights for everyone if we have to.

God's honest truth—we did not have enough money in the account and I was not sure I could get enough in time, but I told Grant that I would—and I definitely would have found a way, if necessary. Thankfully, it wasn't necessary. Grant got the team home without further incident.

The experience was one for the books, at least this book, and became major lessons learned in our growth and maturation process.

While hand delivering hope in the way we do it and the locations we do it in will always require a tremendous amount of trust, these were hard lessons to learn and a scary way to learn them. Don't get me wrong, it could have been much worse, and I am grateful that it wasn't, but I also wish we would have learned these hard lessons without scarring a bunch of generous Changers and losing some others. And I don't know if these will be the last really hard lessons we learn—I sure hope so. But I do know that we did learn from these lessons and have not had a team held hostage in a developing world guest house or police station since.

GUATEMALA

For I was hungry and you gave me something to eat, I was thirsty and you gave me something to drink, I was a stranger and you invited me in, I needed clothes and you clothed me, I was sick and you looked after me, I was in prison and you came to visit me.' "Then the righteous will answer him, 'Lord, when did we see you hungry and feed you, or thirsty and give you something to drink? When did we see you a stranger and invite you in, or needing clothes and clothe you? When did we see you sick or in prison and go to visit you?' "The King will reply, 'Truly I tell you, whatever you did for one of the least of these brothers and sisters of mine, you did for me.'

—MATTHEW 25:35–40 (NIV)

Do you know what your chances of survival are if you are born with a disability in rural Guatemala? Let me put it this way, in Chichicastenango, and many villages like it, there is a hill set aside for the purpose of throwing babies with disabilities over it as soon as the problem is recognized. While this seems calloused and maybe even evil, it is driven by both reality and religion and it is deeply ingrained in the culture. The religious aspect is that disabilities are viewed as a curse or an evil spirit. The reality aspect is that theirs is a life of survival. Feeding your family is hard, and if one of the mouths you are feeding is not attached to a body or mind that can eventually contribute to family survival in the traditional ways as they grow up, then "survival of the fittest" comes into play for them.

There are some families that don't use "the hill approach" and instead they fight, scratch, and claw to find a way to allow their disabled children to survive. Fighting enormous societal, and often family pressures, and pushing against overwhelming financial odds, these families carry their children with disabilities for miles and miles each day to access the very scarce resources available to them. Parents and other family members dedicate extraordinary amounts of time and energy caring for their special needs. Many fashion special carts, beds, chairs, bathtubs, and toilets to help the children function in a very harsh environment, and often "sneak" them extra food or books or clothes in order to help them not only survive, but grow and learn.

One of the very few resources available to them is a very small school for kids with special needs in a wonderful Christian mission center in the hills of Chichicastenango, or Chichi for short. When we first got connected to this group, they were providing education, nutrition, and physical therapy to about twenty kids with special needs whose families said *no* to "the hill." The only available classroom space they had was literally a large storage closet, which made things very difficult to say the least. Still, parents would walk and carry or cart their kids with special needs miles and miles and miles each day to give them the best they could.

By this time in our development, a great lesson we had learned is that *sympathy is not needed or wanted, but empathy is powerful and productive.* We also learned that one of the best ways to develop empathy was by immersion experiences and real cultural exchanges. So, we decided that in Chichi, we needed to interact with some of the families who were walking these miles and miles and miles each day for their kids and visit them in their own homes. We did not walk the whole way from the school to the village—we took vans. But, we did drive by "the hill," which had a similar effect on me as when I walked into the bullet-ridden classrooms in Rwanda. In reality, I could not wrap my head around it. I could not speak. I could only shed tears as I felt my stomach tie into knots, felt all the energy drain from my body, and felt an overwhelming sense of grief and sorrow. Cristi's words in Rwanda rang true again, *"So much bad has happened here."*

The village we were visiting was on the next hill over. The small shacks that the families lived in were built right on the very steep incline of this magnificent, but very rugged and even treacherous terrain. This setting presented our first hurdle for the visit. We had some older individuals with us on this project and we also had Ethan with us, who was in his wheelchair. The vans stopped at the top of the village hill and we all got out and surveyed the scene. The older Changers and Ethan did not want to hold up the group or inconvenience anyone and so they immediately offered to wait there. This did not sit right with me, so I blurted out, "No, we came here as a team to visit these amazing families and we are going to do this as team. Let's form a chain, go slow, and get down to those homes together, okay?"

Like a close-knit football team breaking the huddle for a critical play to win the game, the whole team immediately answered, "Let's do it!" and so we got in place, linked up like a ragamuffin conga line and started our way down the steep hill to the two homes we were to visit. Ethan has incredible upper body strength and can walk with assistance, if two people—one in front and one behind—steady him and help him swing his legs as he goes. So, we started very slowly and then picked up the pace a bit as we all got our rhythm on the descent. It took quite a while, but there were no falls, no injuries, and no quitters. Quite the opposite, in fact, there was lots of laughing, communicating, encouraging, and cheering. And, our "big play" worked, we made it down to the two homes, did a round of high-fives, wiped the sweat off our brows, and smiled big smiles as we saw the radiating smiles that the families had waiting for us as they received us into their homes.

The homes were makeshift wooden structures that appeared to be cobbled together from whatever materials the families could find and fashion into a shelter. The light, heat, and method for cooking was an open fire in the main room of each of the homes, and while there was some ventilation due to the nature of the structures, the walls and ceilings in those rooms were as black as night from the years of smoke. I could only imagine what the inhabitants' lungs looked like. As we always experience with these beautiful souls who have nothing in a material sense, they offered us everything they did have. We had tea and bread. We sat on benches, logs, and the floor and had wonderful conversations (through interpreters) about their childhoods, marriages, families, dreams, children, and dreams for their children. We saw their small gardens and crops. We saw a few pictures that they had of various people and events. We listened, we learned, we felt, we understood, we empathized. Some of this made the grief return, but it also brought a tremendous amount of hope. The hope sprang from knowing that these families said *no* to the hill and were seeing that *"no"* come to fruition for their kids with special needs. *It can be done. It can work.* It seemed very clear to me that our mission had to be to support and encourage these families, and others like them, by providing resources to make it easier, better, and more successful for them and their children. They had just hand delivered hope to us—now it was our turn to return the favor.

The trek back up the eight-story hill was even harder and more treacherous. I put 180-pound Ethan on my back and used a very awkward and comical all-fours climbing technique with some verbal and physical encouragement from the team to make it back to the top. However, when we got to the top, we had way more energy than we did before we even took one step down the hill. The resilience, strength, and purpose of this astounding community filled our tanks to overflowing, and it was an experience that none of us will ever forget.

The first year we worked with this community, we partnered with the mission and another organization to complete two bright and roomy new classrooms designed for students with special needs—and their families. A really special part of that project was that the kids definitely did their part. They worked right alongside of all the Changers to help build *their* school. They shoveled, helped with cement, painted and cleaned *their* school. It was such an extraordinary build and definitely reinforced all we learned about kids with special needs and how wonderfully special they are in so many ways. And, the difference these classrooms made to the students, teachers, and families—physically and emotionally—was more than can be described in words. It is truly immeasurable. It provided a proper learning environment, it allowed for so many more educational activities, and it allowed more individual attention for meeting the needs of each student. Most importantly, it validated the hard work these families did to avoid the hill. It said, *"Your children are valuable, they deserve a quality education as well, and they can contribute to building their school and to their families and communities."* We definitely could not wait to come back and work more with this great organization and these incredible students and families.

So one year later, we went back to help build a playground. *A playground? For kids with special needs in the developing world? Wouldn't there be much better use of time and funds for them?*

Well, we asked ourselves the same questions. And then we did our homework. *Did you know that kids, especially in the developing world, do significantly better in their studies and placement examinations when the school day includes dedicated time for recreation and sport? Did you know that physical education at school improves child health, increases attendance, and heightens social and employment skills?*

We had also learned firsthand from Sam my man, Ethan, and the kids in India that opportunity for inclusion in all aspects of school and life is a key element in a child's development, education, and sense of self-worth. It is a critical part of our mission in communicating the power of education for all people and hand delivering hope to communities around the world.

The final push for this project came from what we observed during our first project in Chichi. The current playground for the center was right near the entrance to the whole complex. So, the kids with special needs would go past that playground each day on the way to their classrooms. They would see all the other kids—and sometimes adults trying to relive their childhoods—playing on swings, the jungle gym, the teeter-totter, or the merry-go-round. The kids—and adults—on the playground always seemed to be having so much fun and getting so much joy from the experience. They were laughing, joking, smiling, and squealing with delight as the kids with special needs would get pushed or carried passed the scene each day.

We were convinced that a special needs playground was actually the very best thing we could do next with the Chichi community, so we took Ethan with us back to Chichi and worked with the kids, parents, and teachers to help them build their special needs playground and garden area.

It was another amazing experience with the kids working hard on THEIR playground and a dedication and celebration ceremony that was profoundly moving and confirming. We think it was a great decision and a fantastic result, but we will let you decide for yourself. Three months after returning home, we received this message from our project partner in Chichi:

Subject: First time on a swing—PURE JOY!!

Dear BTCV,

This morning in the mountains of Guatemala, I found eleven-year-old Joselin Stefani sitting in her wheelchair happily tugging on one of the swings in the "normal kids" playground.

While watching her, I realized that this little girl was probably imagining what it would be like to swing, but her twisted body had never experienced that before.

We talked with her father, Bartalomeo, and he pushed her down the sidewalk to the BTCV Special Needs Playground; we had just the thing for little Joselin. As we opened the wheelchair swing and put the ramp down, her dad pushed her onto the first swing she'd ever been on. Once she was secure, the fun began. Joselin's face was bright with a beautiful smile as she soared in the breeze of her first swing ride.

On that swing, she was "normal," she was "whole," and she was filled with the pure joy that every kid needs and deserves.

Thank you for helping make this possible!

Attached were pictures of Joselin on that swing, with the biggest smile on her face you have ever seen—you could see the pure joy oozing from her whole body. And, you could see the same from her father, Bartalomeo, in the background. A father who chose to go against every cultural, religious, societal, familial, and financial pressure to say *no* to the hill and give Joselin a life filled with education, experiences, love and joy! He is a hero to me.

Joselin's first time on a swing - pure joy!

PERU

We cannot live for ourselves alone. Our lives are connected by a thousand invisible threads, and along these sympathetic fibers, our actions run as causes and return to us as results.

—HENRY MELVILL

There is a tiny little village set on a tributary of the mighty Amazon River called El Chino. This remote village of about 400 people values family, community, hard work, and education. Their economy is driven by subsistence farming and fishing with a small amount of ecotourism sprinkled in. In this part of the Amazon, the river stage rises thirty feet or more during most rainy seasons. As you can imagine, this makes everything in life dependent on the river stage and makes everything quite challenging. This includes building and maintaining schools, and going to school.

The El Chino Primary School was built by the government. Unlike the surrounding structures in the village built by locals on elevated piers, the primary school was built on a concrete slab about three steps up from the ground. The primary school was all the village had for many years, as historically most people in the village did not go on to secondary school based on the prevailing livelihood for the villagers and the need to help sustain the family by getting to work as soon as they were physically capable of contributing.

When I say this village was set on the river, I mean literally right on the river's edge—the river that seasonally rises and falls at least thirty feet (this is not a typo). As a result, the primary school typically would get flooded for weeks to months during the height of the rainy season, causing long gaps in the education the students did receive. Still, this community stayed committed to providing educational opportunities to their children. Many of the children desperately wanted to continue on to secondary school, but the closest one was miles and miles away through the jungle or by river. El Chino is one hundred nautical miles from the nearest road, meaning lots of money to get there even before the tuition, making this option impossible. So, this community found another way. With the help of a local community activist, Dolly Beaver, they converted the village communal building into makeshift classrooms to serve as a secondary school. The structure was rustic at best, had lightweight improvised dividers used as walls between classrooms, and was only slightly elevated and still right on river's edge. Still, Dolly worked with the community to get them to enroll their kids so that they could reach the required student numbers for the government to approve sending teachers to this new high school. So, while it did provide the first opportunity for secondary education in the village, it was by no means consistent, ideal, or conducive to learning. This makes it really hard to get teachers to want to work at this school, which makes it hard for students to get a good education.

Completely flooded school in El Chino, Peru

Then, during a major flood year, the building was heavily damaged, making it nearly unusable. That is when BTCV got connected to this community through a friend of a friend's connection to an ecotourism business. When we got this connection, heard their story, received their application and our board's approval, we sent Grant and a board member for a site visit. During the evaluation process, we learned some good news. The village did have some land available—on higher ground—about a quarter mile back from the river. In addition, Dolly was fully engaged in the El Chino community and deeply committed to their well-being and progress. She turned out to be the perfect community partner who we would very quickly dub as the "Peruvian Wonder Woman." While she does not fit the physical stereotype of the Marvel Comics Wonder Woman, she sure does fit, actually exceed, the using-power-for-good, not-afraid-of-anything-or-anyone, and run-toward-people-in-need capabilities of that superhero. She is maybe five feet tall at best and very petite, but that tiny frame is jam-packed with grit, determination, passion, strength, will, compassion, and love, and she uses it all to help others. She is incredibly loved and highly respected by the entire community. She calls herself "The Jungle's Daughter," which is true, but she should also be known as The Peruvian Wonder Woman, a Champion of Hope, a Freedom Fighter, an Advocate for Education, and a Changer Extraordinaire.

Dolly, aka The Peruvian Wonder Woman, helping to build classrooms in El Chino

As we got to know Dolly during the preparation process, met the community and the community leaders and saw their genuine commitment to education for their children, and did our homework on resources, buy-in, and sustainability, it became very clear that this project was on mission and ideal. We were able to say "*Yes!*" to this amazing community and start on a phased-building total-campus project that is ongoing to this day.

The journey to El Chino is unique, fascinating, and eye-opening in and of itself. Once you arrive in Iquitos, you board a boat on a portion of the Amazon river that is over a mile wide. There are people and boats everywhere. The boats range in size from hand-hewn canoes to large double and triple decker passenger boats to giant freighters loaded with steel, coal, machinery, cars, and/or animals.

The boat we boarded to go to El Chino was a single-decker passenger power boat. The journey is about three-and-a-half hours upriver and the sights you see are incredible. Families paddling canoes along the edge of the river navigating the big boats, fast boats, debris, and wakes. Then, as the river gets narrower and narrower, you see the small villages and the work of daily life on the river—bathing, washing clothes and pots, fishing and playing—and the flora and fauna of the rain forest jungle including pink dolphins, howler monkeys, three-toed sloths, macaws, manatees, river otters, piranhas, pink-toed tarantulas, orchids, rubber trees, and so much more.

The village of El Chino is also incredible in so many ways. It is set right on the bank of the Tahuayo tributary. At the time of year that we visit—the dry season—the village sits high above river stage, about thirty to eighty feet up a very steep embankment. This is amazing to see, but more amazing to think about it being flooded and even more amazing still to see the villagers carrying bags of sand, cement, and rocks and large heavy timbers up incredibly steep and treacherous rough-shod staircases to bring education to the village for their children.

When you make it up the embankment, you see a picturesque little Peruvian village that engulfs your senses such that you fully soak in the culture, community, and connections that are so evident. At the front of the village sits the community center—a thatch-roofed open-walled rotunda, or Maloca, that is the center of village life. The Maloca serves as the social hub, town hall, city hall, dance hall, and most importantly, the "box seats" for the football (soccer) pitch that is at the center of the village—geographically, philosophically, spiritually and emotionally. There is also a church, a general store, a playground, the primary school, and the damaged secondary school scattered amongst the houses of the village. The houses are all on stilts, all with thatched roofs and all of very similar design and construction. The residents include a fair number of chickens, several mange-ridden dogs, and one pig. And, by the looks on their faces, it is really easy to tell that the kids, their parents, the grandparents and the rest of the villagers are all very strong and kind. The first time you set foot in this village, you feel welcome. There are not many resources there, not much technology, and very few modern comforts, but there is plenty of joy, more than enough resilience, and tons of laughter. It is a special place that almost no one knows about.

Importantly, this project began after our failures, mistakes, and lessons had helped us create a defined and proven process, consisting of a formal application initially reviewed by Grant, then by our board of directors, according to organizational bylaws and robust vetting of the local partner, community leaders, accommodations, logistics, travel, safety, and financial components, including required references.

A small team of BTCV site evaluators then travel to the location to experience all aspects of the proposed project firsthand, meet the local partner, community leaders, teachers, parents, grandparents, and kids in person to ensure a shared vision and buy-in, and work together with the community, local contractors, and workers to optimize project design, execution, results, and sustainability. If all the boxes are checked for this process, then the project is voted on by the board of directors to approve, or reject, the budget, timeline, and resources that BTCV will dedicate to the work. *This process works!* It is safe and effective and helps us know and set expectations for the community and our volunteers alike. It allows us to stay on mission, to keep our promises to donors, to *be the change*, and to hand deliver hope in a way that passes the toxic charity and sustainability tests every time now.

The Peru project met the checklist well and completely. So, when the first BTCV team arrived in El Chino, we went straight to the Maloca for introductions, planning, and vision casting—and the vision casting came from them to us—it was a beautiful thing. Even before what the mayor, school board president, elders, parents, and kids said was translated, it was easy to understand the vision, the passion, and the genuine hope in their hearts for bringing the power of education to their village. It didn't take long for everyone to "warm up" to each other. In fact, after the introductions and inspiring speeches, someone from the village grabbed each Changer's hand to lead them back to the secondary school building site. Even though none of us had been there before, it was like we were already part of the community—*we belonged there!*

The trek back to the high-ground building site was the next extraordinary, and frankly unsettling, thing we encountered. It is a little over a quarter of a mile... through very thick jungle. There was a semblance of a path, but it was very narrow, irregular, and overgrown. Four of the men from the village led the way with machetes to help clear the path. Even in the dry season there was a lot of mud and standing water. All I could think about and envision were all the snakes that must be all along that path and how embarrassing it was going to be if I saw one and ran screaming like a young girl all the way back to the boat. Thankfully, I was in the middle of the pack and did not see any snakes on that trip.

When we got to the end of the jungle path, it opened up into a clearing and as we walked into the clearing, it was like the heavens opened up to shine their light on this sacred place and I swear I could hear angels sing. The El Chino community members were so proud and so excited. You could tell that they could already envision their secondary school sitting in this spot—on high ground—and bringing all that it could to their kids and their futures. It was a very special moment.

The first project went very well. The community engagement and commitment to sustainability were compelling. Dolly worked with the community leaders to put a work schedule in place such that each family contributed to the physical work. If they could not, then they had to contribute financially. In addition, each family was responsible for gathering the supplies for and making ten thatches for the roof. This job, in and of itself, embodied our mission because each member of the family participated in it—typically, the father and older kids gathered the wood and branches and the mother and younger kids worked together to weave them into thatches. So, it brought the families together to work on the project and engendered a great deal of pride in the thatches they contributed. Together, the family would typically carry their thatches from the village to the build site in a ceremonious way and set them in a pile to be placed on the roofs. The family would often then stand together until their thatches were placed on the roof, exuding a spirit of pride and satisfaction in their contribution. It was wonderful to see, and so validating in terms of how partnership produces engagement, ownership, and sustainability.

The next special part of the Peru project came when we decided to do "relay teams" for the first time. The phased building plan for Peru entailed a lot of initial concrete work for the pilings and foundation for each classroom followed by all the framing and finishing of the walls and roofs. Well, concrete needs time to cure, especially in the rain forest jungle of Peru, so we really needed to separate the two parts of each build by several weeks or even months. The best solution for this was to send two teams, but we wanted the community and the teams to feel like it was still one effort, one mission, one team. So we decided to split them up but call them "relay teams," which everyone in the community and the organization loved—so much so that it inspired two of our veteran Changers, Pam and Neil, to commit to funding this whole-campus project. We even got a baton with our logo on it to physically pass from team one to the community and from the community to team two and then back to the community until the next year's team one arrived. It has carried on to this day and remains a fun and meaningful tradition.

The next really special part may seem odd to you: toilets. *Did you know that clean and functional separate girls' and boys' toilets at schools in the developing world correspond directly and strongly to improved attendance, better grades, and better scores on national exams?*

This, of course, is especially true for secondary school girls and a big reason why one of the things we love to build most of all is toilets!

So, after two classrooms were in place and the school became very functional, it was definitely time to build toilets in El Chino. Nice, clean, western toilets that were separate for girls and boys—and at the school site, not back in the village. One problem was as much as we love to build toilets, it can be hard to raise money for toilets. People don't necessarily "want their name on toilets" and it can be hard for those of us that have this convenience so available and expected to understand the need and importance of it for kids in the developing world.

But we had a secret weapon in this case. One of our amazing board members, Brian V, is passionate about Be The Change and has a gift for getting people excited about supporting our mission with their checkbooks even when it is for toilets. Brian and his wife, Liz, held a fundraiser at their home in Denver and in one night raised the entire $15,000 needed to fund the El Chino toilets.

And, it was so awesome to see those funds quickly complete their intended purpose that very summer when we did a relay team toilet project. Those toilets were a lot of work, that is for sure. We had to dig a huge pit for the biodigester by hand, do all the trenching by hand, and do all the cement work, plumbing, and construction...by hand. But, boy was it worth it. Each step of the way, I have great pictures of Changers and community members—literally a team of six people standing in the huge biodigester pit that was twenty feet in diameter and ten feet deep, all dug by hand—with the biggest smiles on their faces. There are similar pictures of Changer-Community teams digging trenches, mixing cement, pouring cement, building walls, roofing, and setting toilets—all filled with pure joy...for toilets!

And, then when we unveiled the finished product to the community, it was as if we had just given the keys to a Ferrari to a newly-licensed teenager—it was such a defining moment. Grandkids showing their grandparents how to flush, intrigued dads lifting the seats with their sons. Girls folding their arms and wagging their fingers at boys that were even thinking about coming up the steps to the girls' side. It was a beautiful, joyful scene of people—of different ages, sexes, nationalities, races, religions, and means—standing together, as partners, friends, and family—celebrating toilets in the Amazon jungle!

So, like we said in Guatemala: *yep, a playground!* We said in Peru: *yep, toilets!* In fact, I love to start out my talks with a now-famous line: "My name is Jimi Cook, I am a professor of orthopaedics at a major American university and I *love* to build toilets in the developing world!"

The final Peru story for this chapter is about the Willett Family Bridge to the Future. After three very successful years of relay teams partnering with the community to build three classrooms and the toilets, OG saw another major problem that he really wanted to help fix. The quarter-mile trek back to the school had been turned into a jungle walking path, but that path had to be re-cleared very frequently, and even then it was a pretty tough journey to and from school. More importantly, during the rainy season the students and teachers could easily paddle their canoes all the way back to the school and during the dry season they could at least safely walk all the way back to the school. But during the months between the two seasons, they could not do either as the path was a swampy, muddy, snake-infested mess.

So, near the end of the third classroom build, OG came to me and said, "Jimi, we have to do something about that walk to school for these kids. It's not safe. Can we build a bridge? If BTCV and the community can build it, the Willett Family will fund it."

I told him that I wasn't sure, but that we would get to work on it. So, in true BTCV fashion, we brought Bruno, our amazing Peruvian local contractor, together with Grant, OG, and a new Changer, Ted, who built huge, unique bridges for a living, and put a plan together, raised money, built two relay teams, and went back to El Chino to partner with the community to build a quarter-mile long bridge that was above flood stage. It started at the porch of a new teacher house we also built in the village and continued all the way to the campus clearing, connecting the village to the school. To me, it is the most beautiful bridge the world has ever seen, because it is a bridge to the future—each child that walks on the bridge from the village to the school to get an education is walking toward their future—a better future—thanks to OG, BTCV, Pam and Neil, and an awesome community who is dedicated to helping their children have the opportunity to pursue their education—and their dreams—with passion, so that they can use the most powerful weapon to change the world.

Glenn, aka OG, with El Chino kids on the Willett Family Bridge to the Future

So as you can see, Peru has been incredibly unique, exciting, and very validating for BTCV as it was one of the first that we were able to utilize all our lessons learned, employ our refined methods for application, site visit, planning, organization, fundraising, schedules, timelines, safety, phased-building, community engagement, cultural exchange, and sustainability. *And it sure is working!* No bus trips to nowhere, no bait and switch, no hostage situations, no toxic charity—but most importantly, a true partnership with an incredibly engaged community who is taking ownership of *their* classrooms, teachers' houses, library, toilets, and a bridge to the future to bring the power of education to their community—and from there, the world!

FULL CIRCLE

Once you choose hope, anything is possible.
— CHRISTOPHER REEVE

Remember how this all began? Altruistic travel, kids who wanted books and tuition, a "one-time" school-building project in Rwanda, and people with big and willing hearts who said, *"Yes I'm in!"* and became Changers.

Well, there we were ten years later as it came full circle with us standing in the center of the very same school assembly area where we stood ten years earlier looking at the first school we would work on. Ten years earlier, roofs were caved in, windows were smashed, doors were off hinges, and walls were riddled with bullet holes—right at the chest level of the students. While we, the teachers, the parents and grandparents who survived, and some of the kids, could still vividly picture that scene, the beauty was that the vast majority of the now 1,200-plus student body could not. They only knew the history and the stories about it, because in their lifetimes, Rwanda had been transformed into a safe and flourishing country, and in their time at the school, it was always a beautiful, clean, and well-kept haven of safety, of learning, of a future.

Over the ten years, we had kept in touch, but had very minimal contact with this school in Rwanda. For many of our early projects, our follow-up and reporting procedures were not in place, and our connections did not stay as strong as we had hoped. Thanks to more diligent communication, reporting, and visiting processes combined with advances in and access to technology, we were able to re-establish a strong connection with the Butare School, and *wow* are we glad we did! We were able to come back ten years later—much wiser, more experienced, and even more passionate about education-focused development aid—to help the community build a bigger kitchen, an assembly hall, cafeteria, and a courtyard, and furnish and organize the library. And, this tenth anniversary trip back to where it all began was fulfilling and inspiring. In the ten years since BTCV 001, the Butare Catholic de Primaire School had grown from less than 200 kids and a handful of teachers who were just trying to scratch out some lessons in broken-down classrooms with horrors still adorning the walls to more than 1,200 students and forty-three teachers who have deep pride in *their* school, have not only sustained but grown *their* school, and have completed annual reports to BTCV on their progress showing attendance rates of ninety-five percent or higher, national exam scores in the highest percentiles, and graduation rates that are among the best in Rwanda.

Rwandan students helping to build new facilities at their school 10 years after BTCV 001

They did it! They went all-in as a community to partner with a small NGO to rebuild their past and build their futures with the power of education. They overcame more obstacles to providing a quality education for their kids than most of us could even imagine. But, three women's passionate desire to give back turned into thirty people's willingness to go to be the change, which led to over a hundred parents, grandparents, students, teachers, and community members coming out each day to build classrooms and relationships, and culminated in more than 1,200 kids pursuing their dreams in a safe and encouraging learning environment with the help of committed teachers who have the resources they need to grow young minds. And they, and many others like them from all around the world, are succeeding! BTCV 001 has led to BTCV 050 and counting with more than 7,000 students receiving quality educational opportunities in 17 different countries. Now, that is a beautiful ripple effect, my friends, that I want to keep being a part of—*maybe you do too?*

As I stood in that assembly area with the setting sun giving the traditional dancers the appearance of angelic beings sent to this sacred place as a divine stamp of celebratory approval, it all came full circle again. I heard and felt a strong voice move over and through the hushed crowd. Beata, the Rwandan woman who had escaped the genocide, made a new life for herself through the power of education, and returned home to restore the school that started it all for her, told the enraptured 1,200-plus students, parents, grandparents, teachers, community members, and dignitaries that *they must now Be The Change in the world. They must pursue education with passion, teach with passion, encourage their kids with passion, support and maintain the school with passion. They must strive to be the very best they can be each and every day to improve their lives, their families' lives, the community, the country and the world.* I looked at her silhouette against the backdrop of the library, assembly hall, vocational training center, and classrooms with good roofs, clean windows, and solid doors—and no bullet holes. I couldn't help but beam with joy—true joy, the kind you see on the faces of kids who now have an opportunity, a pathway, a real chance—they have…hope!

So, I'll leave you with that to end this adventure—at least the first ten years of the adventure. I hope that I have told the stories of the adventure well enough so that you can see the beautiful faces of poverty, the children throughout the world who don't yet have, but deserve the opportunities for education that they so richly deserve. And, I will challenge you to be powerful—be the most powerful person in the world—the person who shares that opportunity with those who were not born in the "right" place at the "right" time with the "right" resources.

Remember what Dr. King said, "Darkness cannot drive out darkness, only light can do that. Hate cannot drive out hate, only love can do that." If you, and I, remember that, maybe I will accomplish my BHAG and maybe your story will be part of the next book on the second ten years of hand delivering hope!

Be The Change!

Beata in front of the newly restored Library of her primary school in Butare, Rwanda

Epilogue

"Angry people want you to see how powerful they are... Loving people want you to see how powerful You are."— Chief Red Eagle

To me, *Hand Delivered Hope* is analogous to John Coltrane's *A Love Supreme*. In Mr. Coltrane's words:

I experienced, by the grace of God, a spiritual awakening which was to lead me to a richer, fuller, more productive life. At that time, in gratitude, I humbly asked to be given the means and privilege to make others happy... to inspire them to realize more and more of their capacities for living meaningful lives... I feel this has been granted through His grace. All praise to God.

For Mr. Coltrane, it was music. For me, it is education-focused development aid. For both of us, it is a love supreme!

And again similar to Coltrane, I feel that after these first ten years of BTCV, I can say, *"Nunc dimittis"* (I can die happy now) because the ripple has been started. God willing, I will keep going and accomplish my BHAG, but if not, I am confident that Changers around the world will keep hand delivering hope through the opportunity for education—the most powerful weapon for change and peace that the world will ever know.

And, I am going to "steal" something else from one of my favorite authors, Bob Goff. In his books, he provides his contact information so you can connect with him, promising to answer you directly. I am going to do the same thing here. Email us—we will respond.

Jimi Cook: info@btcv.us

CPSIA information can be obtained
at www.ICGtesting.com
Printed in the USA
BVHW040048300920
589952BV00022B/455